Authors Should SPEAK!

A HOW TO GUIDE FOR AUTHORS WHO WANT TO START USING PUBLIC SPEAKING TO SHARE THEIR MESSAGE AND SELL MORE BOOKS!

by

Dan Blanchard

Granddaddy's Secrets Publishing
Mansfield, CT

© Copyright 2019 by Dan Blanchard

All Rights Reserved. No part of this publication may be reproduced, stored in a retrieval system, or transmitted, in any form or by any means—including, but not limited to, electronic, mechanical, photocopying, recording, or otherwise, without prior written permission, except in the case of brief quotations in articles and reviews.

Cover Design by Tanja Prokop of BookDesignTemplates.com

Published by Granddaddy's Secrets Publishing
Mansfield, CT

Printed in the United States

Library of Congress Control Number: 2019905557

ISBN 10: 0-9862398-3-6
ISBN 13: 978-0-9862398-3-0

Contents

    Foreword

Part 1

1.	Getting Acquainted	1
2.	Priorities	11
3.	Getting Started	21

Part 2

4.	Establishing Yourself as a Speaker Part 1	31
5.	Establishing Yourself as a Speaker Part 2	37
6.	Time to Start Talking	49

Part 3

7.	How to Overcome Fear	57
8.	Pre Speech Fear	65
9.	During Speech Fear	77
10.	Post Speech Fear	85
11.	Where to Find Speaking Opportunities	93
12.	Conclusion	97

Part 4

	Author Speaker Tips	103
	About the Author	117

Foreword

I first met Dan at a Hartford Springfield Speakers Network meeting a number of years ago. He was a ball of fire and I was impressed by his energy and willingness to help others. Getting to know him through the years, I've seen him as a role model for people of all ages and backgrounds. What I love about Dan is that he speaks the truth and lives his message.

During one of our epic coffee chats at Dunkin' Donuts, we were talking about the reality of being an author. Dan said that some people think that once you become an author, it's easy to sell books. We agreed that's not true. As Dan talks about in *Authors Should Speak*, there's nothing wrong with a pat on the back from others and it feels good to get that, but there's a huge difference between getting a pat on the back and someone actually buying your book.

Here's the truth: selling books is hard, especially when you're starting out. With my first two books, I tried a lot of different ways to put myself out there and sell copies. To my surprise, my social media ads didn't bring the return on investment I'd hoped for. Great exposure, but not what I was expecting and I continued to struggle with finding the right avenue for getting my books into the right hands.

After my second book was published, the world thought I was doing great and I received all sorts of praise. Lots of likes and comments on social media. I even got a local newspaper to feature me and the book. But, and this is embarrassing to say, I had boxes filled with hundreds of unread copies of my book sitting in my room. It almost felt like all my work was for nothing.

In a ballsy attempt to get my book out there, I summoned up my courage and started going around door-to-door with copies of my books. In my hometown of Newtown, Connecticut, I literally walked up to people's doors, rang the doorbell, and asked them to buy copies of my books. I got doors slammed in my face, but every now and then I would talk to someone who was somewhat interested. Not the most effective strategy, but in my mind it was better than sitting around doing nothing.

I tried to figure it out on my own and while I had some guts, I wasn't exactly the world's best book marketer.

With my third book, after earning some marketing battle scars with my first two, I like to believe I was a bit smarter. I made a few more connections with people who were willing to help me push the book out to the world. Somehow, with the help of people far more successful than I was at that point, I became an Amazon bestseller in a competitive category. But I still wanted to sell more copies and make an even greater impact.

That's where speaking came in. Everyone tells you the world has gone digital, but nothing beats talking to people face to face. The challenge for me was that I was scared to sell copies of my book after speaking. Despite that fear, some of my most successful days of selling books came from speaking at civic organizations with many people coming up to me afterwards to buy my book. It was an amazing feeling, and it wasn't about the money. It was about knowing that the book was impacting more lives and helping more people.

Even then, I still didn't really have a manual to show me how to approach being an author who speaks. This all changes with this book, *Authors Should Speak*. This is the book I wish I'd had when I started out on my writing and speaking journey. Public speaking is the key to spreading the word about your book, and Dan's book will show you how to do it. It's a practical field guide that's going to help you crush it as an author who speaks.

There's something in here for every author, whether you're at the beginning of your author-speaker journey or you're a season veteran. To this day, I still need to get out there more, and I've found this book to be useful as I continue my journey as an author who speaks. Once you read this book and apply the lessons, you'll be well on your way to getting your book in the hands of excited readers.

Brian Tracy is an author who has written more than 70 books and is considered to be one of the greatest speakers in the history of the world. He endorsed one of my books and I enjoyed connecting with his team. Brian said something I'll never forget too: *"You'll never live long enough to find all the answers yourself. You need to learn from the experts."*

Brian is absolutely right, and Dan Blanchard is the expert who will get you started on your speaking journey. He's lived this as an author who speaks and can guide you every step of the way. The true value of this book is that it will save you the heartache and pain of having to figure it all out on your own. Instead of endlessly poking around in the dark, why not benefit directly from Dan's wisdom and shave years off of your learning curve?

I can tell you first hand, from the bottom of my heart, Dan Blanchard is the real deal. He gets it. *Authors Should Speak* is filled with wisdom that will benefit your author-speaker journey for years to come. He's the teacher I wish I'd known earlier in life. Take this book, devour it, and then get out there and be an author who speaks!

>See you at the Mountaintop,
>
>Jeff Davis – CEO of Jeff Davis International and Amazon best-selling author of
>*The Power of Authentic Leadership*

1

Getting Acquainted

Hello everyone. I'm Dan Blanchard, a best-selling author, an award-winning speaker, an educator, and the author of this book. I am also the author of several other books written on a variety of topics in different genres. I have published both traditionally and self-published, and despite the fact that your book(s) are likely to be different from the books I've written, we're both stuck with the same essential questions and challenges of what to do after our books are published.

Wouldn't it be great if our books jumped right off the bookstore shelf straight into the hands of potential readers? Or if Amazon sent an email to every one of their customers letting them know how great our books are? Yup . . . both of those would be ideal. We could put the challenge of marketing out of our minds and let nature take its course. All we'd need is for a few people to buy our book, read it, and love it. As soon as those first readers started telling their friends and family how great our book is, their friends and family would buy it, read it, love it, and then start telling all their family and friends too. Pretty soon, everybody would be talking about how great our book is and sales would go viral.

It's an exciting prospect that gains momentum with each

imaginary sale. Unfortunately, that's not how it usually turns out. At first, people start congratulating us saying how impressed they are that we've written a book. We're so excited to get such positive feedback that we end up happily giving away twice as many copies as we've sold believing it will get the word out even more. Then, as if time has stopped, our books sales slow down to a trickle—or dry up altogether.

No more book sales? What happened? Everybody was telling us how great our book was. We were earning people's respect too. But for some reason people stopped buying our book.

It's a Process

You might be tempted to think that being an Amazon best-selling author means that I didn't experience this, but I did. Every new author goes through this regardless of whether their book was traditionally published for them, or they self-published it on their own.

But, just as there are many roads to Rome, there are also many strategies authors can use to address the problem of low-or-slow book sales. This book is focused on one particular solution/strategy—publicly and professionally speaking about your books. Yes, it's just one strategy, but you'll get faster results when you focus on one strategy at a time. Master this strategy, and then you'll be ready to add another.

One of the reasons public speaking makes a good first strategy is because you already know everything about your own book. That means that when someone asks you a question, you don't have to worry about knowing the answer!

Is Public Speaking a Good Strategy for You?

Which authors will get the biggest return on their investment with a public speaking strategy? In general, authors who've written non-fiction books based on their expertise. For example, a couple of my books are in the teen leadership genre, but I've also written academic books. All of my books cover subjects I'm a subject matter expert in, so it's somewhat easy to figure out what to talk about if someone asks me to speak to their audience. That might not be the case if I wrote fiction spy thriller novels. People could ask questions, but I'd be limited to how much I could say without spilling the plot. It would be a much shorter talk, and the number of places I'd be able to deliver it would be limited.

Reasons to Consider

One advantage to public speaking is that it can help you find and master your "voice." You've already done it in your book, now it's just a question of getting used to talking and answering questions about it out loud.

I understand that the idea of speaking in public might have you shaking your head thinking that you could never do it, but most people feel like that in the beginning. Like they say, if it was easy, everybody would do it! But this is very good news.

One of the biggest reasons books don't sell is because nobody knows about them. Public speaking is a great way to let people know about your book. And, because an overwhelming majority of authors don't speak about their own books, you speaking about yours puts you miles ahead of them. Speaking about your book will help you professionally too. No matter how you slice it, it's a win-win scenario just waiting for you to step up.

If you need another reason to give public speaking a chance, always remember that there are people who will truly benefit from your valuable content. Isn't that one of the reasons you wrote your book in the first place . . . to share your solutions, information, knowledge, wisdom, strategies, etc.? If someone buys your book, it's because they believe your content can have a positive impact on their life. When someone buys your book, it's because they're ready to improve and/or change some aspect of their lives for the better. Sadly, if they don't know your book exists . . . .

Aiming Your Efforts in the Right Direction

The bottom line is that to sell more books, you need a strategy for effectively and efficiently letting potential buyers know that your book exists. You could continue to spread the word one person at a time, but unless you start talking to people in line at the grocery store, the one-person-at-a-time strategy isn't going to take you very far.

On the other hand, speaking to a collection of people all at the same time is one of best ways to get your book's valuable content in front of a whole group of people at once. And now that you've read this far, congratulations are in order. It means you recognize the potential. It also means you believe in the value of your book when it's in the hands of people who are going to benefit from what you've shared.

You Don't Have to Take This Journey Alone

Who am I to help you on your journey towards using public speaking as a way to increase your book sales? I started public speaking when I took a public speaking class in college.

After college, I joined *Toastmasters International*. Over my years as a member, I delivered over 100 speeches, won numerous speech competitions, and quickly climbed both the speaking and leadership side of Toastmasters. I became the Toastmaster Club President in Plainville, Connecticut, and eventually, the Area Governor overseeing four different Toastmaster town clubs. I even oversaw the Toastmasters Lunch Club at The Hartford Insurance Company in Connecticut's capital city.

I did all of this before I wrote my first book, so when I was learning about public speaking, I had to come up with things to talk about. So you've got an advantage over me right away because you already know what you're going to talk about—your book!

Toastmasters International was a wonderful experience for me, and I can say, unequivocally, that everything I learned through my years as a member and leader within the organization continues to help me to this day. It's a great organization that might be able to help you start your journey with public speaking too, so I really hope you'll check out their website.

How Will You Know?

I'm not sure when I realized that I should start speaking about the books I'd authored. Somewhere along my journey as an author though, I figured out that just writing a book was not going to be enough. Yes, people think it's cool that I'm a published author, and I enjoy the pats on the back. But neither of those has much of an impact when we're talking about actual book sales.

Public speaking can make a huge difference. As a strategy, it isn't new. It's been around forever, and I was very grateful when the connection finally clicked in my head! Once it was there, it was clear to me that using public speaking as a way to promote my message, my content, and my books was an absolute "no brainer" game changer.

The Truth

There's one more thing you should know about me before we get started. I'm nobody special. I'm just this average guy with average abilities who works hard. So don't think you have to have some kind of special hidden talent to be a speaker—you don't. All you need is a belief in the value of sharing your content with more people, and a commitment to giving public speaking a serious shot. That's it!

My belief and employment of this strategy has taken me a long way at this point. Thanks to my books and a little bit of courage, as of this book's writing, I've done over 100 live in-person speeches, and been a guest on over 100 radio and television shows. Twice, television shows liked me so much that they asked me to come back to co-host a show with them. It was pretty exciting being on the other side of the television table as an interviewer instead of being the interviewee.

I worked my way into giving a keynote speech for one of the National Honor Society's Annual Conferences (a society that this former high school "C" student wasn't smart enough to get into when I was in school). I also ran a one-night speaking seminar at Yale University—another place I didn't have the grades or smarts to be a part of.

What I love about both of these speaking engagements was that I spoke as an expert. It didn't matter that I wasn't smart enough to be a member of the National Honor Society or to attend Yale University. What did matter was that I was an expert in my field. That's what got me hired to speak—that and the courage to pursue the opportunity and say "yes" when it was offered. The point being that if an average person like me can speak as an expert at Yale University, you can do something just as equally cool too.

Without a doubt, it's my consistent willingness to speak publically that has helped solidify my status as an expert. And yes, my books sales have increased, which is why I can proudly say that I've been an Amazon Best Selling Author in my category more than once.

Actions

There's little doubt that writing and speaking combined can provide authors with multiple avenues for getting their message out to a bigger audience, which can result in improved book sales. Can I guarantee you improved book sales by reading this book? I wish I could, but I can't. As you go through this book, you're going to read about how to set yourself up for speaking success, but it really does come down to what you "do" versus what you "read."

The strategies in this book require taking action that I can't take for you. In fact, taking action is the first stumbling block most new speakers have to face, so I've included ideas, insights, and strategies about how to get past this, and many of the other stumbling blocks you're likely to encounter. I've also provided you with information and resources for finding and preparing for your first talk.

Are you excited? I am. I know firsthand the value and power of using public speaking as a strategy for increasing books sales, so let's get started!

Part 1

2

Priorities

I'm not even going to try to gloss over the fact that public speaking can be scary. Maybe public speaking ain't right for you—*wait, I can't use the word "ain't" in this book! I'm a teacher. What will people think! What happens if I use the word "ain't" when I'm speaking! That's it! I ain't gonna to speak!*

There's no denying that there's a difference between writing your book and talking about it, so it's understandable why an author would choose to stay within their comfortable writing cocoon. With a book, you have the option of fixing all the mistakes before you publish. On stage . . . not so much. If you say the word "ain't" on stage, there's no way to edit it out. So yes, in that way, speaking is going to take you out of your writer's comfort zone.

Don't Stress Over Being Perfect

Here's a question for you: Are you more comfortable around people who are absolutely perfect in every way, or are you more comfortable with people who aren't always perfectly polished? There's not a right or wrong answer here, it's just that sometimes it's easier to relate to people who aren't perfect.

Obviously, I'm not talking about speakers who make mistakes with their content like delivering the steps of a strategy out of order, or leaving out an entire piece of content. What I am talking about is someone who's a little nervous, or maybe just so zoned into what they're talking about that they don't realize the little things they're doing that aren't perfect.

It can feel downright good to know that even the best and most polished of speakers can still make mistakes. In fact, a few imperfections might make them seem a bit more likable. It means they're human, and that makes them easier to relate to. So don't feel like you have to strive to be a perfect speaker. After all, if you're willing to speak up about your book when it's obvious that you're nervous, then you must really believe in what you're talking about.

Gaining People's Trust

Some people believe that getting people to trust you is a matter of proving yourself. If you're speaking in front of a group or audience, the room itself will help you just by virtue of the way it's physically set up. If the chairs are facing the front, and you step to the front, then people are going to be naturally disposed to listen. We can thank all our years in school for this tendency.

But that's just a habit, and there's no guarantee that the audience is going to trust us just because we're standing in front of them. They might not know us, and if they don't know us, how are they going to trust us? Fortunately, there are a couple of other things that come together to provide the audience with good reasons to trust us.

It starts with us, the author, being clear about what we want our audience to trust us with. For example, I write about teen leadership, which includes publishing two books on the subject. So, if I stand in front of an audience that wants to hear me talk about teen leadership, that's what I'm going to talk about. The audience is ready to hear what I have to say, and in that moment, they trust me to deliver the content they came to hear. I trust that they're open to hearing what I have to say. Being on the same page is a great way to start building trust.

Staying on the same page is also where it's easy for new speakers to get sidetracked—especially when it's the result of a great idea or thought popping into their head while they're in front of an audience. It's so tempting to go off on a tangent or to start ad-libbing content. Between our ears it feels like the perfect addition to what we're talking about . . . right up to the moment when we start talking about it and realize we don't know how to put it into words. I hope reading this is enough to keep you from making this mistake. If your new idea is truly a good one, you'll remember it and can add it in for the next time you speak. Until then, stick to your script! Don't learn this lesson the hard way!

As long as you stay on topic, deliver your content in ways your audience can relate to, and can answer people's questions, you're well on your way to earning your audience's trust. The result is that people are more likely to accept you as an expert and your book as being written by an expert—both of which will be good for book sales AND opening up more opportunities for speaking gigs.

I Know . . . It's Still Scary

As you read this book, you're going to notice that some of the ideas are written about more than once. That's because fear can be a big issue, and it wouldn't be fair of me to think that you're going to read something once and then ***poof!*** your fear of public speaking will be gone. Nope, it doesn't usually happen like that.

So, my goal as your speaking coach is to keep giving you information, inspiration, and steps you can take to tackle the problem head on. Because the truth is that if you want to sell more books and make a difference in this world, you're going to need to get out there and talk about what you're doing. Why? Because people are more willing to accept the content you're sharing in your books when they can attach a face and/or a voice to a message that's captured their interest.

Non-fiction is really different from fiction in that way. Fiction authors can be successful without anyone ever knowing who they are. With non-fiction though, people want to know more about the person. It comes back to that trust issue. A person might write a really great book on how to lose weight, but if they themselves are extremely overweight, it's going to be very hard for a reader to accept them as an expert. And who can blame them! That's why today's readers want to know something about the person behind the name that's written on the book's cover before they're willing to pay for the book.

You've Already Started

Let's think about what you've already accomplished so far. You've written a book! I bet there was a time when you didn't think you could do that either. Before you started writing, your book was nothing more than a thought, an idea, or a dream. Then you started writing, and word by word, your book took shape. You saw it through and now you have a book.

To me, that's evidence that you can do what you set your mind to. With public speaking, it's just the job of setting your mind to it. The benefits make it easier to think about too. It's cool when people consider you an expert. It's also fun to sign books for people—especially when they buy them from you after they've heard you speak.

So technically, you're more than half-way on your journey to becoming a speaker because you've already finished the really time consuming part—writing the book.

Brand You!

Another thing you've accomplished with writing your book has to do with building your "brand." Everybody is talking about branding these days. What is a brand? It's simply you providing people with a way to distinguish you from others in your field of expertise.

Take a field trip to a book store and go to a non-fiction book section on a topic you know nothing about. As you look at all the books on the shelves, there's not much to see beyond a bunch of book spines with different titles. How would you make your decision on which one to buy? You could pull each book off the shelf and read the back cover and the table of contents. You could read the blurb about the author too—which hopefully includes a picture. Will that be enough information? Will you have to look at every book before you make your decision?

Now consider this: What if you've heard the author of one of those books speak and you really liked what they had to say? Would that make a difference? Of course it would!

When you wrote your book, you started building your brand. When you start speaking about your book—even if you start small—you'll be adding another way for people to recognize you and your expertise. This is a process known as "building brand recognition" and it can have a very positive impact on your book sales.

Multiplied by Three

In today's world, you need to give people as many opportunities to find you as you possibly can. You're off to a great start by taking advantage of the first multiplier—writing a book. This accomplishment has already launched you into a category above your competition. You've increased your visibility, and as soon as you start speaking you'll be taking advantage of the second multiplier—your voice.

You've probably heard the idea that the more of a person's senses you can engage the more likely they are to remember you. As an author, you engaged their sense of sight when they read your book. When you start speaking, you'll be engaging their sense of hearing. The third multiplier comes into play when people begin to recognize you based on all three of your brand components: the expert, the author, and the speaker.

This is when people begin to recognize you and say things like: "Oh yeah, I heard him/her speak—great content!" Your readers want to feel like they know you, and it helps them know you better when they read what you've written and then hear from you in person, on the radio, the TV, and/or the internet.

The more opportunities you give people to remember you for all the right reasons, the more likely they are to trust that buying your book is a good investment. And let's not forget the possibility of them deciding to do business with you too! And yes, it feels great to share your valuable content, but it's okay to be rewarded financially for your work too. Think about it this way . . . every dollar you make represents you using your expertise to help someone.

How Long Will It Take?

Every time you put yourself in a position to be both seen and heard, you're increasing your audience and building brand recognition. The reason this is important is because there are a lot of people vying for the attention of your readers. The wrong way to deal with this problem is to try to be "better" or more visible than the competition. When you're focusing on how to excel over your competition, you're wasting time and energy that could have been used to build a better relationship with your readers. The right way to deal with competition is to be consistently persistent and authentic when you interact with potential readers.

In marketing terms, they call those types of small interactions with customers "marketing touches." In the early days of brand building it didn't take many touches to get someone to take action. Sadly, because not all business people have the best of intentions, the number of touches it takes to get someone to do something—like buying your book—has risen dramatically. Again, this doesn't mean that you have to do a better job than anyone else. It's just a reminder that if you don't give people a reason to remember you, they're going to forget you simply because there's just too much competition for their attention.

This is where public speaking, once again, comes into the picture. Online, it might take eight to ten touches—probably delivered by email—to inspire someone to buy your book. That's a tough way to build a relationship! But when people sit in your audience, they get to hear you and see you in action. Being in the same room with you helps them get a better sense of who you are. It also makes it easier for them to decide if they know and trust you enough to buy your book and/or do business with you after you're done speaking.

Your Courage Muscle

There are people who will say "feel the fear and do it anyway." Even I'm tempted to say this every once in a while, but I would never say it to someone who was just getting started with something as big and scary as public speaking. What I can say is that this book is going to help you build your courage muscle one step at a time.

If you think about it, your courage muscle and your fear muscle are basically opposite sides of the same muscle. You can't feel courage and fear at the same time. You can go back and forth really fast between the two feelings though, which is what happens to someone when they're about to do something they're really afraid of—like bungee jumping (which I've done). In situations like that there's no doubt that the fear aspect of the muscle is screaming at them not to do it. When someone manages to take that first big step though, it means the courage side was screaming louder.

In this book, I'm sharing thoughts, ideas, and strategies meant to increase your awareness of the courage side of this muscle so you can use the trick of letting your courage cancel out the fear. And even though you might be shaking your head and thinking that it can't be done, I hope you'll keep reading so you can discover that it really does come down to simple strategies. And yes, building up your courage muscle is definitely going to help you sell more books!

Back to Writing Your Book

I want to give you a concrete example of what happens when you start paying attention to the courage side of that muscle. Before you started writing a book, you probably had some fear about writing it. *What if I can't write . . . What if my writing is really bad ... What if people don't say good things when they read it ... What if I start and can't finish ... I don't have enough time to write a book ... Nobody knows who I am, so why bother?*

You might not have had all those fears when you were contemplating writing a book, but you had some of them—everybody does when it comes to writing their first book. But instead of letting your fears stop you from taking those first steps, you figured out a first step that wasn't too scary and you took it. I know this is true because you wrote (or perhaps are in the process of writing) your book. Here are a few more relevant examples of things we were afraid of until we did something to manage the fear rather than letting our fear continue to manage us.

- Do you remember learning how to ride a bike? Most of us were afraid we'd fall and it would hurt. Once we got the hang of it though, it was a piece of cake.
- How about the first time you drove a car in traffic or on the interstate?
- How terrified were you the first time you talked to someone you had a crush on?
- Were you shaking in your boots just before your first real job interview?
- How old were you when you finally stopped being afraid of the monster under your bed or the boogeyman in your closet?

Each of these examples had a fear component that was very real at the time we were experiencing it. But as soon as we learned enough to get over them, we just forget that there was a time when we were afraid. The good news is that if we can do it once, we can do it again. And yes, the fear of public speaking might rank right up at the top, but that doesn't mean there aren't easy steps and ways to navigate it. *(Notice how I didn't say get over it? I'm not going to ask you to get over it. I'm going to share steps you can take that will keep you squarely in the driver's seat rather than the other way around.)*

3

Getting Started

Let's lay out a straight-up truth here. The only thing stopping most people from starting to speak in public is fear. Everything else about public speaking is completely doable. I could sugar coat this truth, but that's not going to do you any favors. Better to just say it like it is: There's always an audience, and always content worth sharing. So it's not like speaking is something you don't have a choice about. You do have a choice. What you need is a better understanding of how to recognize and deal with the fears lodged between you and your desire to speak.

Let's Put This in Perspective

In the last chapter I mentioned the idea that courage and fear occupy the same space. That means that you're either flexing your courage muscle or your fear muscle. Think about what happens when you're stuck in fear. It's fight, flight, or freeze, and when you're stuck in one of those feelings it's almost impossible to think or feel anything else. When you're on the courage side of the muscle, it just feels better . . . freer. You don't run from the idea of taking action. You feel more excited, maybe exhilarated, and quite possibly, a bit braver.

With public speaking specifically, this means that if you aren't focused on the fear—i.e. all the reasons you can't speak in public—you're able to focus on what you can do. So let's begin by tackling one of the most common fears people have about public speaking—not having anything to talk about.

I already know this isn't the case with you because you've written a book, are in the process of writing a book, have outlined a book, or collected all the material for a book. You might have even started writing your next book!

You have content. Chances are that you have content beyond your book too. And yes, this book is about using public speaking as a way to get the word out about your book, but I want to remind you that you can use public speaking to share any kind of content. This means that if you're a business person with lots of content but haven't written your book yet, you can still follow all the advice and information in this book to grow your business.

Book or no book, you have content . . . content that's worth sharing because it will help people. Your steps, no matter how small they may seem to you, do make a difference. Our world becomes a better place when each of us adds our positive and intentional steps. We amplify the magnitude of our steps when we write and/or speak, which has the great side effect of increasing our book sales and our business.

All of this means that you don't have to worry about having something to say when you speak. Your head is already full of great and valuable content that people will be happy to hear and learn more about.

Why Would Someone Want to Hear What You Have to Say?

This is one of the easiest questions to answer: Because not

everyone has figured out what you know!

People are busy, so busy that they rarely feel like they have the time to stop and figure things out. When you think about it, this is why advertising works. It reduces our need to think. We go to a store, look at a selection of items, wonder which one is the best, remember a TV, radio, and/or internet commercial we saw or heard, and grab that brand name.

This is very good news. It means that when people are sitting in your audience they want to hear what you have to say. They're ready to learn from you so they don't have to do all the hard work of learning what you already know. When people sit in your audience, they are sincerely predisposed to hearing the content you're going to share. This all boils down to a simple fact: You don't have to convince people that you have content worth listening to. They will know that before they sit in your audience because they'll already know what you're going to talk about.

What Should You Talk About?

Considering that this is a book about how to use speaking as a way of increasing book sales, my first obvious answer is to speak about your book. But that doesn't mean it's the only thing you can talk about! Are there topics in addition to your book that you're passionate about? If you have other subjects and topics you'd love to share with an audience, find that audience and let them know you'd like to speak to them about this topic.

Think about activities that float your boat when you're not at work. What subject can you talk about for hours without getting bored? Do you have a hobby or talent you excel at? Is there a topic people are always coming to you for advice about? Is there a topic you wish more people knew about?

Speaking about another topic might result in you becoming a sought-after expert in that particular topic too. You might even be able to use your knowledge in this topic as content for your next book.

Having a book is definitely a great source for having something to talk about, and it's definitely the best place to start. Just keep in mind that if you have another topic you could speak on too, people who liked what you had to say on a different topic might still be inclined to buy your book.

The Gettysburg Address

The one thing I would warn against is speaking about everything to anybody. No speaker can be everything to everybody. The problem is that once you know what you want to talk about, it's very tempting to create the biggest, flashiest, most comprehensive speech on your chosen topic that anyone has ever delivered. I know this can happen because I have to keep reminding myself about this while I'm writing this book!

I would love to write one book that addresses all your questions about writing, publishing, and speaking, and about how they all come together to complement each other. But then I think about something like the Gettysburg Address. It was only 272 words long (depending on which version you read) and it's one of the most memorable speeches ever given.

Adding more words is rarely the answer. Neither is trying to prove that you're a "jack of all trades" expert when it comes to your topic. The people who come to hear you speak are interested in the specific topic you said you were going to speak about. Don't be one of those speakers people tune out simply because it took you too long to get to the point. Instead, do yourself a huge favor and stick to your chosen topic. Deliver on what they came to hear you talk about and you'll have given them a reason to say good things about you after the fact.

Niching Your Book Down to a Topic

If you've written a book that has more content than you can cover in the amount of time you have to speak, you'll need to decide how much content you can comfortably share. Start your decision making process by listing reasons why people would want to read your book.

For example, one of the reasons a teenager might read my teen leadership books is because they want to figure out how they can start taking charge of their own life. Obviously though, there's no way I could talk about everything I covered in those books in one talk. Instead, I'll pick one, two, or three specific points (depending on who's going to be in the audience and how much speaking time I have) that are both valuable and actionable. That way I've given them enough information to take action even if they haven't read my book yet. I've also given them a choice. If they like what I've talked about so far, they can purchase my book when I'm done speaking. Or, they can try out the "free" content I've shared from the stage first and buy the book later.

Another way to choose content is to think about what your audience's pain points are. If you have a way to reach out to them before the event, you might be able to send out a short email inviting them to tell you what they'd like you to talk about. You probably know where your clients hang out online too. Check out the groups they belong to and see what they're talking about. If you're already social media savvy, check Facebook, Instagram, and Twitter too. Wherever your audience is hanging out, meet them there and find out their problems.

In addition to deciding what content you're going to share, make sure you know enough about your audience to "meet them where they are." This is kind of a variation on not trying to share everything you know in one speech. This time I'm referring to our tendency to feel like we have to justify our right to speak to the audience. We all want to feel like we matter and might do things without realizing it—like talking over people's heads or making things more complicated than they need to be. The solution is simple . . . don't do it. Don't talk over people's heads. Don't go for flashy or try to wow them with how great you are. Let your content be the star and your audience will know that you care about them.

How Much Content Should You Give Away?

We've all heard the words "the whole truth and nothing but the truth." It's part of the statement people swear to in court. Okay, maybe I'm being a little dramatic here, but if you're going to share content with an audience, it's important to make sure you share enough information for people to understand it and/or take action.

Too many people get scared about sharing their information because they think that once they share it, no one needs to buy their book. Once again, you're never going to have enough time to share everything that's in your book. But let's look at this concern from a different perspective . . . how easy is it to learn how to do something in one sitting? It isn't. You didn't become an expert overnight, and no one in your audience is going to become an expert just by hearing you explain something to them once. That means that people who want to understand your content on a deeper level are going to buy your book, or maybe even approach you directly about working with you.

There are really only two reasons why someone wouldn't be interested in learning more about you, your book, and your work if you've made good decisions about what and how much content to share:

1. They were never going to buy your book to begin with simply because they never were and never will be a good fit for your content.
2. You held back on the content so much that you didn't give them enough information to get to know and trust you and/or your book.

You don't have to give away the "farm" when it comes to sharing your content. You do have to give the people in your audience a good "taste" though. Look at it this way . . . if you were looking for a place to have dinner and walked by an Italian restaurant with a waiter standing outside handing out samples of bread and butter, would that be enough information to get you to go inside? Good bread is really good, but it's just not enough.

Don't hand out "bread" to your audience. Give them a hearty sample of the main course. Not so much that they're full, but definitely enough to wet their appetite for more.

Part 2

4

Establishing Yourself as a Speaker – Part 1

One thing that's definitely going to lessen your fear of public speaking is addressing your status as an expert. There are two parts to this. Part 1 has to do with what we think about ourselves and our status as an expert. Part 2 has to do with what the audience thinks about our status as an expert. This chapter is about the process of accepting ourselves as experts within our specific topic.

What is an Expert?

I went to the internet and googled the word "expert." The definition that popped up was: *A person who has a comprehensive and authoritative knowledge of or skill in a particular area.* Not exactly a scary definition . . . except maybe for the word "authoritative," so I looked that one up too: *Able to be trusted as being accurate or true; reliable.*

That's not scary either. All it's saying is that an expert is: *A person who has enough knowledge and/or skill within a specific topic to be considered a trusted resource when sharing their knowledge and/or skill within their topic.* It doesn't say anything about being the absolute best or ultimate authority, guru, or any of those other overwhelming titles that leave us feeling like we're never going to measure up.

There is never just one expert within a topic. I don't care what the topic is, there's always going to be someone who knows more than we do. I'm willing to bet that every person reading this book knows of at least one expert who's more knowledgeable/skilled than they are within their topic.

I recently tossed my hat in the local political arena and was elected to an entry level political zoning position. If I didn't have confidence in my knowledge and ability to take on this challenge I'd never have pursued it. But there's no way I would claim that my political "expertise" is equal to the expertise of people whose whole lives revolve around politics! The point is that you don't have to be the #1 expert in the world to be an expert for your next audience.

Remember that most well-known and respected expert speakers started out right where you are now. They had reasons to speak in the beginning too, and had to figure out what to talk about and how much content to share so that their audiences would start accepting them as an expert in their topic.

The Self-Judgment Trap

We are so human sometimes that it can be downright frustrating! One of our long-standing tendencies is to think that other people are judging us—especially if we're speaking to them from the front of a room. And okay, yes, they probably are sizing us up ... but they aren't actually thinking about us when they're doing it. They're thinking about themselves and whether or not the information we're about to share is going to help them. That's what they care about. They're investing their time and energy and they want to get something of value in return.

This is good news because it's totally within our control to choose content we know is going to help the people in this specific audience address at least one of their problems. We know this because we've done our homework—more than our share of homework in fact. So much more homework that we know more about our topic than a large majority of the people around us. In other words, between our own ears, we are beginning to accept ourselves as an expert. The challenge is letting other people know we're experts too. The reason it's a challenge is because it's so easy to fall into the "self-judgment" trap.

In case you don't think this could happen to you, here's a question: Are all famous speakers beautiful or handsome? Of course not. Are all famous speakers perfect speakers? Nope. They're all human just like we are, and it's that human part of us that's afraid because we don't feel like we fit the stereotype of someone people would be willing to both look at and listen to.

When we believe in the content we're sharing though, and our goal is to help as many people as we can by sharing our content both with our book and from the stage, our perspective begins to change. We don't have to think about ourselves as the center of attention, or worry that people are going to pay more attention to the zit on our cheek than they are to the content we're sharing. Speaking isn't about us or how we look or sound. It's about the quality of the content we share. When we get comfortable with that distinction, we are free to get into how awesome it feels to share information, knowledge, wisdom, strategies, methodologies, etc. with people—content that carries the potential of changing some aspect of a person's life for the better.

It means we can take the spotlight off of ourselves and shine it directly where it belongs, onto our content. We believe in the value of our content. We believe in the value of sharing it. Sure, we hope that we'll benefit monetarily by sharing it too, but we believe in our book because we believe that sharing it directly with people can literally change someone's life for the better.

Our job as speaker-hopefuls is to make the shift from worrying about what people will think of us over to believing in the value of our content. When we do, our confidence in ourselves as experts in our topic and content shows, and our audience is more likely to take both us and our content seriously.

The "Please Pick Me!" Trap

When you've written a book that you really believe in, it's easy to get excited talking about it. But when your book sales start to dry up, excitement can sometimes lean towards desperation, and that's when we start saying things like: "It's a great book ... really ... your people will love it ... I promise!" Even if every word of that is true, it's going to sound more like begging than anything else.

I get it. If you could just convince someone to give you a chance to speak, they'd be thrilled with the result. But getting an invitation to speak is a negotiation, and begging is like blinking first. If you were going to buy a car, you'd probably have to talk to a salesperson. When you talk to the salesperson, you're going to be asking questions about the car. The salesperson pretty much knows the questions you're to ask and is prepared to answer them.

It's basically the same when you approach someone about

speaking to their group. You're going to be asked questions about your book so they can decide if **your** content is going to work with **their** audience. If this sounds a little bit like the self-judgment trap you just read about, that's because there is some crossover here. The real distinction is that you'll be having this conversation with one person instead of an audience.

The best way to prepare for these conversations is to make sure you're prepared to answer all their questions about the topic and content you'd like to speak about. Write out questions you think people will ask and come up with answers to them ahead of time. You'll be amazed at how much easier it gets to talk about your book with practice.

*****

Believe this or not, it can get pretty magical when you start talking about and sharing your content with people. When people "get it," they smile and nod their heads. They come up to you when you're done speaking, say "thank you," and ask you to sign your book for them. It's very cool. It can be humbling too, to know that you're in a position to help people. Most people work their entire lives without any direct awareness that they've genuinely helped another human being. That's when speaking can become downright addictive!

5

Establishing Yourself as a Speaker – Part 2

It's time to talk about ways to encourage people to accept you as an expert beyond you announcing you are when you're asking them if you can speak to their group/audience. Gotta confess that this is a bit like trying to convince someone to hire you for your first "real" job. As long as you continue to build your reputation/brand though, people will begin to accept you as the author-expert you say you are, and will eventually start asking you to speak to their audience before you ask them.

The problem is that speakers who are just getting started are darn near invisible to people looking for speakers. But here's a news flash, even established experts can be invisible when it comes to being asked to speak. Why? Because they haven't put any time or energy into letting people know that they're available and interested in speaking. All they'd have to do is follow some of the advice I'm sharing with you in this book and then they'd have people calling them and asking them to speak too. It boils down to building up your creditability as an expert.

Building Your Credibility

Be consistent with your content. One of the first things people are going to wonder is if you are as invested in your topic as you say you are. This is an easy one—keep writing about your topic of expertise. Writing articles, blog posts, tweets, books, etc. is going to help you build confidence in your ability to talk to anybody about your topic. The more written content you have, the more likely people are to find you too. Each piece of content is further proof that you really care about helping people. There's also the advantage that the more you write, the better your writing will become.

Let people know that you have a solution for their problem. Experts are people who see problems and come up with solutions for those problems. One author-turned-speaker who did this is Robert Kiyosaki. In his book *Rich Dad Poor Dad*, one of the wealth-building solutions he wrote about was the unique idea that people should stop thinking of their home as an asset, and instead, see it as a liability. This "twist" was definitely controversial, but his unique ideas and creative problem solving got people's attention, which helped him sell a lot of books and make a lot of money speaking . . . which naturally led to more chances to write and sell more books from the back of the room when he spoke, as well as over the internet.

Your solutions don't have to be as unique or controversial as Robert Kiyosaki's, but your content does have to solve legitimate problems. For example, speaking about the best way to do laundry probably doesn't sound as if it's going to solve a real problem. But, if your book is titled "10 Steps to Becoming a Bonafide Adult," and one of those steps is learning how to do laundry, your unique twist might be that learning how to do laundry is a stepping stone to taking control of how you dress and look in public, which could increase the odds of people being more comfortable around you.

Don't underestimate one person's struggle when they don't know what to do in the face of their problem. It doesn't matter if it's a small or big problem either. Once people have a solution that works, they are so relieved! Now they can cross that problem off their list and move on to better things.

Don't stress yourself out thinking that the content you share with your audience has to provide life-altering solutions either. People love simple solutions too, so keep this in mind when you're writing articles, blog posts, etc. that will help you get found by the people struggling with the problems you have solutions for.

Don't rely on the idea that your solution will fall into the right person's hands at the right time. Like I said, it's unlikely your book is going to fall off the bookshelf at your local bookstore right into the hands of your ideal reader. The same goes for all the additional writing you've been doing. If people don't know about it, the chances of them finding it on their own are pretty slim.

The simple solution is to make sure the people who already know you also know how to find your new content. After all, people are busy and aren't going to have time to plug your name into a search engine just to see if you've come up with something new. With people who've already given you permission to email them, send a short email letting them know you've got some new content to share. You can post on social media too. Remember to include the link to the content to help them out—they're busy people!

There are actually many things you can do in this category, but again, I don't want to overwhelm you with all the possibilities. Just trust me when I say that getting your work in bigger and better places where more people can read it is not as hard as it probably sounds right now.

Give people a chance to get to know you. Now that you're getting your content out, you'll want to make sure the people reading what you've written have a chance to get to know you too. This is easily done by writing a short-but-great bio to accompany everything that gets published, both in print and online. It's worth it to put some time into this too because you want people to get used to seeing you and your content together.

Start by writing a general bio. When you're happy with it, take that version and edit it down to a shorter version, and then edit that down to an even shorter version. This way, you'll know which version to use based on how much physical room there is for your bio, or how many words/characters you're allowed.

It's easy to think that every new article or presentation needs a bio written specifically for that occasion, but over time it's only going to leave people wondering if you're the person who wrote that other post/article. It's okay to update your bio to add a new credential or something like that. Just don't keep changing it. Be consistent. Then, when something you've written resonates with someone, your bio will give that person a chance to learn more about you, which makes it more likely that they'll remember you.

Another reason to be consistent is because people want to know if you truly believe in your own message. Consistently showing up and talking within your expertise is evidence that you do. For example, it would be a stretch to trust your dentist's solutions for getting the best resale price for your car. I'm not saying your dentist wouldn't know how to do this,

I'm just saying that trusting him as a how-to-sell-your-car expert is going to be a stretch. Being consistent with small things like a bio will start earning you people's trust.

Choose topic titles that clearly state your theme. For example, a title like: "The Recent Increase of Women in Politics" provides clear information about what the speaker would be speaking and presenting about. An event planner looking for a presentation on politics, women, gender, and/or leadership might consider this speaker a good fit.

Too many authors go for cutesy titles that may sound amusing but don't provide enough information. A title like: "Women Wearing Political Power Suits" is too vague. In a planner's mind, if your title is vague, there's a chance your content might be vague too.

Your titles can be interesting and maybe even fun. Just make sure that the theme of your presentation comes through loud and clear. Well thought out titles are memorable too—which comes in handy when a planner is looking for a speaker and someone mentions you and the memorable title of your presentation.

Advanced Strategies for Building Your Credibility

None of the above ideas or strategies is going to stretch you too far out of your comfort zone. In fact, some of them might sound so logical or simple that you'll be tempted to dismiss them. But they're important when you're getting started as a speaker. They are the groundwork for your speaking, and each one of them will help you build a solid foundation for your speaking platform.

Doing a good job with the items listed above is also going to prepare you for more advanced strategies. Think of them as learning how to walk. I know some people would rather run first, but in general, you want to master walking before running a 25k race. That being said, here are a few advanced strategies—just in case you're one of those "runners" . . .

Always be on the lookout for ways to get your expertise and work out there. If we're already doing this, there are definitely ways to kick it up a notch. Be willing to serve as a contributing expert on a panel. Be willing to answer people's questions. You'd be amazed at how many people will ask you if they can buy a copy of your book right then and there! (Which reminds me, make sure you have copies of your book stashed in the trunk of your car, your briefcase, your backpack, etc.)

Feed your articles and blogs to the market. Sending your articles, posts, etc. to family, friends, and social media acquaintances is a good place to start, but it's not going to help you grow beyond the circle of people who already know you. Remember that there is a virtual flood of content these days. One way to stand out is with great content because most of what people put out there isn't very good. So doing even the basic stuff, like trying to make sure there aren't any typos in your work will put you leagues ahead of the people who don't care. Unfortunately it won't matter how great your content is if you don't get it in front of the right people.

If you want to increase your reach, you'll want to start identifying people to send information to about you, your work, and your book. Before you start calling or sending anything to people who haven't "opted in" to hearing from you though, do some research so you don't step on anybody's toes by mistake. There are definitely protocols and strategies for increasing your success rate with this kind of cold-emailing. The most important being to remember that people don't like "spam." And even though you don't think of your work as spam, if it shows up in someone's email box uninvited, that's how they're going to label it. The reason this strategy falls into the advanced category is because getting labeled as a nuisance or spam is no joke.

Another reason why I added this advanced strategy is because it's never too soon to start making a list of people you'd like to reach out to.

Continue to build your platform both off and online. There might not be absolutes when it comes to what a platform consists of, but there are components to a platform that will help you enhance both your reputation and credibility.

- A website
- A blog
- More written content such as ebooks, Kindle books, pdfs, and articles
- A media kit and marketing materials
- Joining a speakers bureau

The reason this is advanced is pretty clear. It takes time to pull all these things together, not to mention the fact that you might not need all of these things depending on how much speaking you want to do.

Figure out where your peeps are hanging out both in person and online. If you have a solution for someone's problems, you probably already know some of the groups and places they hang out. But it's a big world and you might be pleasantly surprised at what you find when you start doing some legit research. Make sure to start a list of what you find. If you're online and you come across a group or a person that sounds like a good fit, don't stress over what to do right that moment. Instead, open a blank word document and title it as "contacts" or "research" or something that makes sense to you. All you have to do now is copy and paste the names, information, links, etc. into the document. That way you can do a lot of research all at once and then go back and start weeding through it later.

The advanced part of this strategy is how to start engaging with groups, forums, people, etc. Most groups are easy enough to get into, but you don't want to get into the habit of joining groups with the intention of getting your book in front of them. If you do decide to join a group, get to know them and let them get to know you. Start contributing to conversations other people have started before starting conversations of your own. Be respectful.

As with all these advanced strategies, there are protocols to follow so do some research before jumping in without a proper invitation. Do this right, and you'll have the opportunity to win them over. Win them over, and they'll spread the word about you and your book. Your reputation will grow—in good ways—and that will help you sell more books and get more speaking gigs.

Become a reputable and quotable resource for other experts and authors. There is a real power in being quoted, and there are many people who would love to have someone to quote! Just imagine the opportunities that might open up when other experts and authors are mentioning your name in their content or when they're on stage—which, of course, can lead to more book sales. The reason this as an advanced strategy is because to put yourself into positions where people might quote you, you have to get out there with your quote-worthy content, and that means networking—with a twist.

Everybody wants to be quoted, and being quoted by other reputable experts and authors is a great way to extend your reach. But be selective about who you say "Yes! You can absolutely quote me" and/or who you're going to ask "Can I quote you on that?" This is another advanced strategy where research comes into play. Go online and figure out the names of the experts and authors in topics and niches that are close, but not exactly the same as yours.

For example, if I wrote a book about the how-to's of running for a local political office, I probably wouldn't ask the person who was running against me for a quote about losing. On the other hand, I might be able to get a great quote from someone who has been rising through the political ranks. I could also talk to campaign managers. (Hmmm . . . I might have to give this book idea some more thought!)

Do some research before you say, "Yes, you can quote me on that!" to someone you don't know much about. Always make sure you're clear about the context of how your words will be used too. The same holds true for asking someone if you can quote them . . . do your research!

Become a contributor to high-level platforms. Publishing your content on your personal blog is terrific, but well-paid speakers are expected to be contributors and content writers on larger platforms too. One of the biggest advantages to publishing your work on someone else's larger platform is that you get your work in front of a whole new audience of people. It's going to do wonders for your credibility too!

Getting people to accept you as a contributor takes work though. This is where the consistency I've been harping on comes into play. The more content you have out there, the more likely bigger platforms are to consider you.

The advanced parts of this strategy are the protocols and how-to's of approaching other people's platforms. I've had success with reaching out a couple of times. If you check out the testimonials on the front and back covers of my books *The Storm* and *A Sprint to the Top*, you'll see some big names. It wasn't like I called or emailed them once and got the testimonial I was hoping for though. Nope. It took time, patience, respect, and consistency on my part. In the end, it was worth it, and it's worth it for you to have a good strategy in place instead of just reaching out willy-nilly.

I know there are people who've just made the phone call or sent the email and got the response they wanted immediately too. But that's not a strategy you can count on for the long haul. Besides, a good strategy is more likely to increase your odds of getting someone to say "yes" the first time.

Let's Slow Down for a Minute

I have a feeling some of you are probably stressing right now, and the last thing I want to do is overwhelm you with all these advanced ideas. But I have to be straight up about what's possible with speaking. It's kind of a "the sky's the limit" adventure, because speaking can get addictive. There's nothing as great as seeing people responding to what you're saying to them. It's exciting because if they're responding, it means you're succeeding with your goal of helping them. What's better than that!

That's why I shared some of what you "could" do if and

when you decided that you wanted to share your content—and your book—with bigger and bigger audiences. I've seen it happen more than once, and it definitely happened to me . . . but that doesn't mean it will be the same with you. You might decide that you don't want to do any of the things I mentioned above and that's fine. You are definitely not required to become a "big-time" speaker. In fact, how big you want to be is entirely up to you.

Building Relationships

Most of you already know the value of building relationships. Relationships can be tricky though, like when there's an undercurrent of competition. The good news is that your book makes you unique. Writing your book wasn't something you did to thumb your nose at your competition. Your book is simply your content/message delivered from your perspective. This makes both you and your book unique, which means you can start building relationships without worrying about what anyone else (a.k.a. the competition) thinks!

I've already talked about Toastmasters International, but I'm going to mention it again because this is one of those places where you can start building relationships. You just never know who you're going to meet, how they might be able to help you, or how you might be able to help them.

Look around for speaker's groups in your area. I found a great one about an hour's drive from me. It was filled great people all coming together to learn more about the "business" of speaking.

There's just no getting around the advantages of building relationships with people, and even though you probably already know this, I'm going to add it here anyway. Building relationships is more than shaking hands and exchanging names and phone numbers with someone. Sadly, there are people who forget this and judge potential business relationships from a "what's in it for me" perspective. Don't be that person.

*****

That's it for building your status as an expert, your reputation, and your relationships. It's not the last I have to say on any of those subjects, but it's time to move on to finding those first speaking opportunities, securing a gig, and getting up on stage!

6

Time to Start Talking

I'm going to start changing gears here and talk about actually speaking. So far, we've been skirting around it covering ideas and information about how to set yourself up for success. But if you don't actually start speaking, you're not going to be able to enjoy how good it feels to have someone shake your hand and thank you for writing your book. Trust me, signing books after you've spoken cannot be overrated. Every handshake means I've contributed something of value to someone else's life. Every book I sell has the potential of improving some aspect of someone's life.

The sticking point is that you actually have to start speaking if you want it to happen. Right now though, I'm going to focus on "talking" rather than speaking. Believe it or not, an excellent non-traditional avenue to getting started with speaking, or at least beginning to build your speaking muscle, could be talking to the media.

Finding Your Voice in Private

One of the simplest ways to get practice with "talking" is by being a guest on someone's podcast. Not only is it simple, it's not too stressful when you're getting started. You'll most likely be talking on your phone, being interviewed from the comfort of your own couch. There's usually no video or face to face going on so you can even be interviewed in your PJ's if that's going to make you feel more at ease.

Another reason being interviewed for a podcast is simple is because your conversation is going to be taped, which means it probably can be edited too. That way, if you make a mistake or would like a "do over," the podcaster should be able to accommodate. Phew! You don't have to be perfect!

If you're not ready to do research to find podcasters who would be a good fit for you and your book, another option for getting some talking practice is radio. Some radio stations will schedule a phone interview. Others will invite you to come to their studio to be interviewed. But even if you do go into their studio, there's not going to be a physical audience.

The good news is that both podcast and radio personalities are going to do everything they can to make the interview a success. Why? Ratings. They want people to listen to their shows, which means they're going to use their skills to help you relax and feel comfortable during your conversation with them. So you don't have to worry about them letting you flounder or just plain throwing you under the bus. On the other hand, if that happens, it's proof that you need to do better research! As I've mentioned before, do your due diligence before saying yes.

One notable difference between podcasts and radio interviews is that podcast audiences will probably be smaller and maybe even more targeted. Radio programs have a bigger audience that might not be as targeted, but it's probably going to include people who might recommend you to someone else after hearing you talk. *"Hey (person who's been looking for a speaker) . . . I heard a radio interview this morning about (you* and your topic). The person they interviewed wrote a book about it. The title is (your book's title). You should check it out."

Developing your one-to-one conversation skills and tone will help you lay some groundwork and prepare you for future speeches in front of a room or up on a stage. The audience will love it when your speech sounds more conversational too—like you're just talking to a friend. Some people might even feel like you're talking directly to them.

Finding Your Voice in Public

There are other ways to start getting used to "talking" too. These aren't the same as delivering a presentation from a stage, but they will get you used to speaking in front of a group.

- If we're still in college, be the first one to volunteer when everyone in the class has to stand up and present a project to the whole class.
- Volunteer to coach a youth sports team, and you'll be in plenty of situations where you're going to have to talk to both the kids and/or their parents in groups.
- Volunteer to work with youth clubs. With clubs, you might not see as many parents, but you're still going to be talking to a group of kids looking at you for guidance.
- If you're a parent, volunteer to help in your kid's classroom, and to speak about what you do when the opportunity presents itself.

The bottom line here is to look for opportunities to speak to people so you can get some practice talking while people are looking at you. Practice is the key ingredient to becoming a successful speaker, so keep looking for those opportunities!

Getting Paid to Speak

I know you're wondering about how speakers get paid. The truth is that when you're starting out, getting paid isn't normal. Generally speaking, speakers have to work their way up the *getting paid* ladder. The two components planners use to decide whether or not they'll be willing to pay are 1) how recognizable you are as an expert, and 2) how much positive speaking experience you've had.

Of course, even if you don't get paid, you have a huge advantage over other unpaid speakers—you have a book to sell, and that's definitely going to take the sting out of not being paid. The reason I'm bringing this up now is because when you're willing to speak for free there are so many more groups you can approach. (I'll share more about these groups later in this book.) For now, just know that there are opportunities to speak in a lot of places you'd never have thought of.

Recently, a woman told me about a conversation she had with one of the bank tellers at her bank. The opportunity presented itself, and because she just happened to have a copy of her book with her, she showed it to the teller. The teller asked her if she ever spoke about her book. When the woman said yes, the teller told her that they have a meeting room people can use to give presentations and such, and that the bank would promote her and her presentation—and she could sell her book.

No, she wasn't going to get paid. On the other hand, she found an opportunity to speak about her book—and sell it—in front of a group of people without having to pay anything for the room. It was one of her first speaking gigs and it went great.

Try not to worry over getting paid when you're getting started. Get started and keep working on building your speaking skills. Remember that the goal isn't to get paid... it's to increase your book sales. The more books you sell, the more people you help, and that's going to feel really good. This, I know from experience.

Authors Should Speak!

Part 3

7

How to Overcome Fear

Let's start this second part of the book by pulling another one of those tough truths right out into the open. If your books aren't selling, the only person who's going to care is you. But don't start thinking that the reason it isn't selling is because it isn't a good book. If your book isn't selling it's because people don't know about it. If they don't know about it, how can they buy it? Easy answer . . . they can't.

It doesn't mean they don't want to hear about your book either. There's a whole audience of people your book can help. That's why you wrote it in the first place. But again, if they don't know your book exists, it won't matter how good it is or how much it could help someone. If they don't know about it, they won't buy it.

Good. Now that we've gotten that reality out of the way, we can skip right to remembering the biggest reason why you need to get over your fear of public speaking—to help people. Once you start thinking about all those people, it will be easier to tackle your public speaking fears. More people will know about your book as a result, which in turn will lead to sales.

The interesting thing about the fear of public speaking is that it can be broken down. If you think about it, most people just say, *"Oh, I could never speak in public because I have a fear of public speaking."* But that's just a general label. For example, some people might experience more fear before they step on stage. Others are okay until they're speaking and suddenly start feeling the symptoms of stage fright.

First Fears First

One very helpful thing to know about many of our fears is that even though they can feel very real, most of the time they aren't. Real fear is the fear that's going to inspire you to take—or not take—an action so you won't get hurt. For example, if you were standing at the edge of a cliff, your heart would probably be pounding. You might be shaking and maybe even be having a hard time breathing. That's a legit fear response that will hopefully keep you far enough away from the edge that you don't fall off. That kind of a fear response helps you stay safe from harm.

A person who has a fear of public speaking could have the exact same physical reaction just by thinking about speaking. And when they're experiencing that fear, it's hard to convince them that there isn't any real danger because it absolutely feels real to them in that moment.

Real fears, like the ones that actually keep us safe from harm, play an important role in our lives. Fears that aren't real don't help us; they just hold us back. Some of those fears, like the fear of public speaking, come with a steep price—they limit the number of people we can help.

Fortunately, fears like the fear of public speaking can be broken down. The first place you can break it down is with saying something to yourself like: *"Okay, yes, I'm afraid to speak to a group, but that doesn't mean I can't takes steps forward as if I'm not afraid. How do I know I can't do it? I've never had this good of a reason to work on it before now. And maybe, if I take it one step at a time, I'll be able to do it. One thing's for sure . . . if I don't try taking at least one step in the right direction, I won't know if I can or can't. And if I don't at least try, it's like I'm letting down all those people who could really use my help."*

Sometimes it's easier to be strong for others than it is to be strong for ourselves.

How Simple Silly Fears Become Great Big Fears

Remember when you were a kid and you were afraid there were monsters under your bed or in the closet? Or maybe you were afraid of the dark. Sometimes the fears we pick up as kids can stick around for a long time and genuinely keep us from living our best life—the life we deserve to live. They might start out as simple small fears, but if nothing happens to change them, over time they can morph into bigger adult-sized fears.

You might expect me to say, "Feel the fear and do it anyway" right about now, but I'm not going to. Instead, I'm going to walk you through some of the things you can do that will make the fear go away on its own. Think of the ideas you're going to read as turning on a light in a totally dark room. Once the light goes on, everything you thought you were hearing or seeing suddenly makes sense. The only truly scary things in the room were the thoughts and fears running through your mind. As soon as you see that there's nothing to be afraid of, the fear just disappears.

When it comes to your fear of public speaking, there's probably a lot of the fear of the unknown going on. For me, that means turning on a bunch of lights. And I know your fears feel very real to you right now, but that's just because they've been a part of your life for a long time. They're a part of the way you see things. Just keep reminding yourself that even when a fear feels completely real, that doesn't mean it is.

So, let's combat those phony fears by becoming more aware of our false fears and accepting that we don't have to allow them to control us. They're just fearful thoughts and feelings about public speaking that we've collected over time. That's all. They're not real. We are not our thoughts and feelings. We are our awareness of our thoughts and feelings. And once we start paying attention to our negative thoughts and feelings about public speaking, we're in a position to help our brain pay attention to what's really going on.

This is how we begin to stop letting our fears stand in our way. We start replacing unfounded fearful thoughts about bad things that might happen with positive thoughts about what can happen when we plan our steps forward. It's like Henry Ford said:

> ***"Whether you think you can or you think you can't, you're right."***   ~ Henry Ford

Taming Those Big Speaking Fears

When you think about the big public-speaking picture, it can look pretty overwhelming. But public speaking is like anything else you're going to do in your life. If you have a plan, and you keep taking action, you're probably going to accomplish your goal. The trick here is to figure out which fears are getting in the way. And even though it may sound scary, the best way to start exposing those fears for what they really are is to expose them to the light of day by writing them down.

I know you can write them down because you've written a

book. In fact, I'm willing to bet that in your book you did something very much like what I'm doing here—you used your expertise to help other people overcome their fears about dealing with their struggles. Okay, maybe there isn't a lot of fear involved if your book is about something like: *How to plan and execute the perfect family vacation without tears or residual credit card debt.* On the other hand, going into debt is a huge fear for many people. It might be the single biggest reason why someone has never taken a real vacation in their entire life!

The point is that you already have experience addressing **other** people's fears. Here, in this book that I've written for you, my goal is to help you overcome your fear of public speaking so you can increase your book sales.

Some people believe they can **think** their way through their fears. Unfortunately, trying to think through your fears doesn't work very well. As soon as you start thinking about a fear, that fear can get triggered and take over. Writing about your fears is an excellent strategy for not getting caught up in endless thought loops of fear and negativity that might push you down rabbit holes of even more fearful and miserable thoughts.

I'm not saying you have to write a book about your fears or that you need to fill a huge journal. I am saying that as soon as you start writing about them, they start losing their power over you. On paper, they just aren't as big or bad. On paper, they can't do anything. They are nothing more than a collection of words just laying there. They're powerless, and it gets easier and easier to realize that they aren't real. The only real existence a fear can ever have is the existence you give it when you let it take up residence in your mind.

The second part of this strategy is to start editing the images your brain conjures up when you're thinking about doing something it doesn't think you should do. You see, images are a shortcut your mind uses to convey a lot of information at once. When you start attacking your fears on paper, your brain is going to take that shortcut and start filling your mind with pictures of why it's right, trying to convince you that what you're writing is wrong.

This is one of those times when you can take a stand though. What you're trying to do really matters—you're trying to share your great book with others. To do that, you're going to have to start taking steps that will challenge the fears that have been holding you back. I know you can do it because I've done it. In fact, human beings have been doing this throughout our entire existence. If they hadn't, it's doubtful we'd be here. And trust me, if I can do it, anyone can do it. I had to get past my fear of public speaking too. I still get nervous before I speak (and I'll be addressing that issue shortly) but I refused to let it stop me from helping others, and you shouldn't let your fear stop you from helping others either.

Fight, Flight or Freeze

Now's the time to get a good handle on the pictures your brain is tossing into your mind's eye. Remember, your brain's goal—which includes both fearful images and thoughts—is to keep you safe from harm. It uses fear to inspire you to fight your way out, to run away so you don't get caught up in the danger, or to freeze so that you become invisible to the danger.

But seriously, how likely is it that you're going to be facing any actual danger talking to people about your book? Are the people you're going to share your book with likely to put you in any of those positions? Nope. Why would they? You're offering them information which they are free to choose or not choose without repercussions.

When we start looking at the fear of public speaking from these perspectives, it gets easier to see it for what it really is—an overinflated idea that does nothing but create havoc in our lives. Like most false fears, all it does is hold us back from living our best life, which is the life we deserve to live. These fears are not real. So let's dissolve them in the light of day and stop them from putting limits on the good we can do!

Let's be grateful for our ability to have written and published our book, and for the ability to speak about it too. I can tell you from personal experience that gratitude is like a superpower. The great ancient Roman orator Cicero called gratitude the mother of all other virtues. It can pull our thinking off of ourselves and our problems and help us focus on the good that is continually going on around us, as well as the good that our message adds to the world. It feels good to look at what we're doing from this angle. Our sharing is actually helping make the world better—even when it's just one reader at a time. That's reason enough to be grateful for what we've already accomplished, and for what others might be able to accomplish with our help.

8

Pre Speech Fear

Now that you're beginning to get a grip on your fear of public speaking (at least enough to keep reading), these strategies are going to help you make sure you're fully prepared to speak. For example, one thing some people fear about public speaking is that they're going to forget what to say. The simple solution is to decide what you're going to speak about way before you speak.

What Will You Speak About?

Everybody's answer to this question is going to be different because everybody's book is different. What is the same for everybody is the need to come up with an outline of what they're going to speak about. Outlines are awesome! They help us stay on track, which makes it easier not to stress about saying every single word perfectly, which then helps us speak from the heart of our desire to share our content with our audience.

The real challenge with creating an outline is not *what* to talk about; it's *how much* to talk about. Rest assured that no one's going to expect you to talk about your entire book. Your job is to narrow down the scope of your book into a select group of talking points.

One way to decide what content you're going to share is to think about sitting down and talking with one person—the one person in the world your book could help the most. You get to share one, two, or three ideas with them, and you have 20 minutes to share it. 20 minutes—that's it! Yes, that sounds limiting. But if you share those ideas well, the people listening to you are going to want to know more, and will be more likely to buy your book.

I bet the wheels in your mind are turning and you're thinking, *"But I can't share my best stuff with them when I'm speaking! If I do, they won't need to buy the book!"* Don't worry. This is one of those fears that's going to disappear as soon as we pour some light on it.

It's hard for people to remember exactly what you say no matter how good their note-taking skills are. On the other hand, if you don't share some of the good stuff, they won't have a reason to take notes. So don't be afraid to share some of your best content. I'm not saying to share all of it, but do share some of your best. That alone will "wow" many people right into purchasing your book!

F.E.A.R—False Evidence Appearing Real

The real power of starting with an outline is that it's going to erase another fear—the fear that people won't be interested in listening to what you have to say. The truth is that they will be interested. In fact, they want to hear what you have to say very much. It's not like the people in your audience all have the time, energy, and money to go out and do all the research you've done. This is one of the reasons why speakers are in such high demand. As knowledgeable expert-authors, when we speak we are literally saving the people in our audience time, energy, and yes, money . . . and they know it.

I'm pointing this out because it's a perfect example of how a fear can feel so real and yet be nothing more than *F.E.A.R.— false evidence appearing real.* It's easy to think that a fear like "no one's interested in hearing what I have to say" is real when there's no evidence to prove it false. But there's plenty of evidence to dispose of this fear. People do want you to share your expertise with them. Consider the popularity of TED and TEDx talks.

Now, I don't know if you're ready to think of yourself as a TEDx speaker yet, or if that's even a goal. I just know that all those TED author/speakers were once in the same exact place as you are now. They had to come up with an outline. They had to remind themselves that their books were good books that could genuinely help people. So, instead of fearing that no one wanted to hear what they had to say (F.E.A.R.) they focused their thinking on how many more people they could help when they started speaking. It worked for them, and it can work for you too.

Another fear about to bite the dust is that even with an outline we're going to screw up. LOL . . . even the best speakers in the world can make mistakes when they're speaking. We're all human. None of us is perfect, and forgetting to say something, skipping something we wanted to say, losing our place, etc. is stuff that happens to all speakers. The cool thing is that when it comes to speaking, the only person who knows what we were going to speak about is us. Nobody in the audience knows, which means they won't know we made a mistake if we don't tell them. So don't tell them. Just keep going.

And while we're at it, let's expose the fear of rejection:

"What if my audience hates my speech? What if they boo me off stage?" It's not going to happen because you're going to know about the audience you're going to be speaking to, so you'll be able to plan accordingly. You know better than to talk about the virtues of being a Red Sox fan to a room full of Yankee fans. You know better than to intentionally antagonize the audience. Make either of those mistakes and the audience might boo you off the stage. But now that we've put this fear in perspective, it's not a problem.

You know who President Franklin Delano Roosevelt (FDR) was, right? He said, *"You have nothing to fear but fear itself."* He was right, and let's extend that thought. Think about the false fears we've talked about so far. Now that they've been exposed, they don't have the same amount of power over you. If you hadn't read about how to expose those fears to the light of day though, you might have lived the rest of your life without sharing your book as much as you wanted to. The only thing real about F.E.A.R. is its ability to blind us from recognizing true opportunities. The only real product of any F.E.A.R. is regret.

Step by Step

You're on a roll now. You've got an outline worked out. Have you found your first speaking opportunity yet? It's not a big deal if you haven't. In fact, now you're in an even better position to start letting people know that you'd love to speak to their group or at their event. You'll be able to confidently tell them that you're an author and that you'll be speaking about your book. All that's left to do is to determine the date!

Here are more things you can do to keep your confidence growing between now and the date of your first speaking engagement:

Practice, Practice, Practice! I can't say this enough, but I don't want you to think I'm saying you should memorize your speech. Well, maybe the opening and closing so you have it down pat. TED Talk founder Chris Anderson encourages speakers to memorize their openings and closings, but says that the rest shouldn't be memorized and should just flow naturally.

Practicing your speech before you get on stage is what's going to help it flow out of you naturally. The way to start practicing is by making sure your outline matches what you're going to talk about. Start speaking it out loud. If you're going to be standing when you're speaking, make sure to practice standing. Keep practicing in a way that's as close to the real thing as you can make it and your confidence will continue to grow. And remember, you'll always have your outline as a safety net.

Get to know your audience – Obviously you won't know everything about them, but it's easy enough to get a sense of who will be sitting in your audience. Ask the person who booked you for information about the people who will be in the audience. Ask someone you know is going to be in the audience about them. If it's a group, check the internet to see if they have a website or a Facebook group.

Knowing about your audience ahead of time makes it a whole lot less scary. They're coming to hear you speak so they'll know a little bit about you too, and then it will be more like a group of people who have something in common getting together.

Deliver your speech to someone – This is a great way to practice in a non-threatening environment. If you know someone who can be both objective and supportive, that's the best situation because you're more likely to get positive and constructive feedback. If the person is too invested in supporting you, they might shy away from pointing out things that could be improved.

Don't limit yourself to doing this once or twice and thinking that's enough. Do it as many times as you want or need. Each run-through is going to help you get caught up in the natural flow of your topic. Because you're practicing on different days, it might sound or flow differently. But that's okay. Each run-through will add to your confidence and then, on the big day, you'll feel like you've already been there and done that.

Practicing "as if" – I'm sure you've heard the old saying: "Fake it until you make it." First, remember that you're an author/expert, so you're actually qualified to be on stage. Second, if you've done a good job of preparing to speak to this specific audience, then your audience is going to accept you as an expert, which means you won't have to fake it. You are a legitimate author/expert with a book and content to share. The more you practice with these realities in mind, the easier it's going to be to get over another F.E.A.R. it's time to expose: the "imposter" fear.

For some people it's not enough to know that they have the credentials to speak. Instead they fall into that feeling of *"Oh no! I'm an imposter! People are going to see right through me. They're going to find out that I'm nothing special"* before they step on the stage. Those ideas are nothing more than F.E.A.R.-generated self-sabotaging thoughts trying to convince people to keep playing it small, and that it's safer for them to stay within their comfort zone.

But hey, putting ourselves out there is a good thing! Remember, you're the person the audience is ready to learn from on that day. You're the person they will come to see. If you don't show up for them, that's like giving them permission to continue to play it small and safe too—not a good thing. You getting up there in spite of your fear is proof to them that they are worthy and that they have a right to reach for something better too!

So don't let the F.E.A.R. that you're an imposter freak you out and sabotage your happiness and success when you start speaking. Push those fake voices right out of your head. Replace them with the voices of real people thanking you for speaking to them and sharing your expertise with them. Bring in thoughts of how much they will benefit, and it will be even easier to get into the flow and push your comfort zone out just a little bit further.

If you're going to use a PowerPoint, practice with it – PowerPoint (PP) is a great tool. For one thing, it gives your audience something to look at besides just you! It can help you stay on track too, but be careful not to just read the slides word for word to the audience. They came here to listen to you speak, not to listen to you read. The problem is that it's easy to become so reliant on a PP presentation that some speakers look at it every single time they change a slide to know what to talk about next. Then, instead of the PP being a benefit for the audience, it's become a crutch for the speaker.

That doesn't mean you can't use your PowerPoint presentation as a reference. Just remember the advantages of a piece of paper with your outline on it too, and keep that paper handy because technology doesn't always work. Not only that, when it doesn't work, you're still going to have to speak! How stressful would that be if your confidence was based on having the PowerPoint to follow!

The good news is that you're learning this lesson right

now so you don't have to end up learning it the hard way. Definitely practice with your PP, but make sure you can deliver your speech both with it and without it.

Get Organized – Now that you've got your speech planned out, make sure you've got yourself organized and ready for the event. Get a box with a lid and put everything you think you're going to need or want when you're at the event into it. Make sure to include some "just in case" items too—like extra copies of your outline and introduction!

Getting a Grip on the Approaching Stage

As you get closer to the event, it's time to think about some of the things that happen to you when you get nervous. First though, please notice how I said *nervous* here instead of scared or fearful. There is a difference. When it comes to nerves, there are a bunch of quick and easy mental and physical things you can do. If any fears come up, well, at this point you know they're false, so there's no need to think of the fear of public speaking the way you used to. Instead, remind yourself of how F.E.A.R works, kick those negative and limiting thoughts to the curb, and start working on calming your nerves.

I guess I can compare the scary walk to the stage with something that happened before every football game I played in. When we were lining up for the opening kickoff, we were all nervous. The kicker kicked the ball and every player on the field sprinted down the field with everything they had in anticipation of the game's first hit. You know what I found out time after time? It got a lot better after that first hit. Even with everyone watching us, that long run downfield and the first hit of the game settled my nerves down, and that's when I started enjoying the game I loved to play.

The same sort of thing can happen for speakers when they're taking that long walk onto the stage and finally speaking their first words. Being nervous is normal, and as speakers, it's up to us to figure out how to make our nervous energy work for us, instead of against us. Here are some tips I put together to help you deal with your pre-speech nerves:

Work on your breathing – If you tend to have a hard time breathing when you're nervous, go online and find a strategy for breathing that will work for you. One simple way to deal with it is to take slow calming deep breaths with your eyes closed. It's almost like a mini-meditation that will relax you.

Exercise before speaking – This works well for people who build up a nervous energy before they speak, but is dependent on how much time is available. For example, if you like to jog, you could go for a jog before getting ready to head out to the event. If you're at the event, maybe a vigorous walk outside will do the trick.

The good thing is that when it comes to exercise, you're in complete control. It's just a matter of making sure to manage your time so that you're calm and collected when it's time to speak. Well . . . at least as calm as can be expected of any speaker because most speakers are nervous before they speak.

Meditate on a daily basis – Mediating will help you stay calm. It will center you and help you better identify what's important and what's not. And trust me when I say that fear is not important—not mine . . . not yours. What you're preparing to speak about is important, and taking a few minutes a day to calm your thoughts about speaking by meditating is going to help that truth settle and calm you from the inside out.

Reduce your stress by practicing being stressed – Elite athletes do this all the time. Before they hit their "stage," they close their eyes and visualize the positive outcome they want. But they don't just do it before they're about to perform. They visualize while their training and working out too. They imagine what it will be like when they succeed, but also what they'll do in moments of stress too.

It's the persistent practice that makes the difference. So don't wait until the day before you're supposed to speak to start visualizing a successful presentation. Start visualizing stepping on stage when you're practicing. Don't avoid any nervousness that comes up. Instead, acknowledge that it's there and then come up with your own personal strategy for overcoming it. Then you'll be prepared for any nerves that show up just before you're supposed to start speaking.

What Do I Do When I Get Nervous?

When I get nervous, which I still do, I take deep calming breaths and remember what I read about John F. Kennedy (JFK). People said that JFK wasn't that good of a speaker, but what made him special was that he always looked like he was having fun when he spoke. He looked as if he enjoyed the podium and his time with his audience. And I'm pretty sure this made people think that he was not just a better speaker, but maybe that he was better looking than he really was. Hey, what can I say, it's a process that works for me.

So let's go ahead and put on our good-looking smiles. Let's laugh a little bit (if it's appropriate). Let's imagine having a positive impact from the stage and give ourselves permission to feel good about being where we are—even when we can feel our comfort zone being stretched. Trust me . . . it will make you better looking to the audience. Who doesn't want that!

9

During Speech Fear

You made it. You really made it. You're standing in front of your audience and you have every right to be very proud of yourself for this accomplishment.

Now what . . . because I'm not going to lie, the first few times you get up there, it's scary. So let's start by dealing with those scary thoughts right here and now. What's the worst thing that can happen when you're suddenly all alone on the stage? Are you afraid you're going to:

—Forget everything you were going to talk about? Easy fix . . . you've practiced your beginning and ending enough that you practically mumble them in your sleep. You've got your outline too, which means you have easy access to what you're going to talk about next. In fact, you've got backup copies of your outline on your phone, in your email, and a couple of print copies stashed in a couple of different places. You won't need them all, but it's definitely reassuring to know they're there. Even as soon as when you finish your first talk, you'll have more confidence in what you're talking about. Eventually, you won't be as dependent on your outline or your PowerPoint.

—**Stammer and stutter?** This one is totally about nerves and isn't as likely to happen if you get in some quality practice in front of a few people rather than waiting to "practice" in front of a live audience.

—**Forget something really important?** Once again... OUTLINE. Also, there's a big difference between forgetting and not knowing. This is your stuff and you know it! And, again, you have your outline to keep you on track.

—**Faint, throw up, or freeze on stage?** Professionals deal with these feelings all the time. The difference is that they've learned to manage them. Eat a few hours before getting on stage. That way you'll be fueled but not full. If it works for you, physically move around before and while you're on stage so your muscles won't have a chance to tighten up. Of course, the biggest thing to remember, the one that's going to make all the difference in the world, is to remember to breathe.

You're laughing aren't you... don't. Have you ever been in a situation where you practically stopped breathing but didn't even realize it? It happens. So feel free to take a couple of steadying breaths as you take your place.

Again, the first couple of times you step on stage can be tricky. Reminding yourself of why you're in front of this audience is always going to help. You're there to help the people you're about to speak to. You're there to share something meaningful. You're offering something in good faith, and it's going to feel better each time you step on a stage because of it.

Just as importantly, be proud of yourself. You've done a serious amount of work to get here and now you're positioning yourself to be able to enjoy the rewards of your labor—more book sales!

Start Easy

Thinking about standing in front of a lot of people is one of the reasons people get so nervous about speaking. The easiest way to deal with the pressure of a bigger stage is to start with a smaller one first. If you've never spoken before, then even 12 people sounds like a lot. So don't start there. Start with an audience of five first—or even four.

Smaller audiences make it easier to get comfortable with things too—like knowing that everybody is looking at you. It's so much easier to start with having a few people's full attention focused on you rather than a room full of eyes.

A small audience makes it easier to practice breathing and making eye contact. Eye contact can be tricky because it's hard to know the difference between too little, too much, and just right. The goal is for enough eye contact to let the audience know you're looking forward to your time with them. It's also an opportunity to see them and realize that they're looking forward to their time with you too.

Decide What Feels Right

Do you know how quickly you speak? Did you know that talking too fast can interfere with your breathing patterns? Yup. Talking too fast can actually make you feel panicky all on its own. Every time I watched JFK speak, or any other presidents, I notice that they always speak slowly. Hmm ... there must be a good reason for that s-l-o-w talk if all of our presidents do it, right? So do a little research to figure out how fast or slow you talk. Decide the pace that feels comfortable and natural for you, and you'll naturally be calmer and more relaxed when you speak as a result.

Can you speak from your heart? Very few things are as engaging as a speaker who clearly knows the power of what they're sharing. I'm not suggesting you break down in tears as proof. But it's okay to let people know that you're speaking because you sincerely want to help them improve some aspect of their life. Another advantage of speaking from the heart is that it rarely requires a lot of practice.

How's your posture? I know . . . you're laughing again. But there have been many studies done on the power of standing straight and tall—aka the Superman/Wonder Woman pose. When you take that stance, it actually sends signals to your brain that increase testosterone levels in both men and women, which leads to increased feelings of confidence. These stances also lower cortisol levels, which reduces anxiety. I'm not suggesting you should strike the pose while you're on stage, but you can definitely practice at home and prove to yourself that it works. Then, find a way to power-pose in private before you take the stage. Hey . . . if it works . . . .

Have you practiced your smile lately? I know there are speaking topics that don't exactly call for comedy, but that doesn't mean that while you're on stage you have to look like a stodgy old professor imparting his ultimate cure-all wisdom for what ails you. Even with tough subjects, there are times when your smile can be reassuring to your audience. Your smile can reduce your stress level too.

*****

I suppose I could have listed all of these earlier in this

book, but they all require experience before we can appreciate them. At the very least, you'll be able to name what you're experiencing when one of them pops into your head the first time you take the stage. Once you master them, you won't even give them a second thought!

Getting Pulled Out of Your Speaker Zone

Even when you're fully prepared, looking out and into the faces of your audience for the first time can be unnerving. So it really helps if you can connect with at least one friendly face. It might be someone you've personally invited to hear you speak, someone you were in contact with prior to the event, or someone you met before you took the stage. It can even be someone who just looks friendly. Whoever it is, it always feels good to know there's someone in your audience who's genuinely interested in what you have to say.

Don't be surprised to see someone in your audience paying more attention to their cell phone than they are to you. The first time it happens it's likely to distract you and bring up the fear that it's your fault they aren't paying attention. But maybe something very important is going on in their life that you don't know about. Whether there is or isn't, don't let yourself get distracted by the false notion that it's your job to figure out how to keep every person in the audience interested for every minute of your talk. It's not. In fact, it says a lot more about the reality of how easy it is to become so dependent on our devices that some people can't go without them for even 15 minutes!

A deeper reason why some people might give into distractions while you're sharing information from a book that can help them (or someone or something they care deeply about) is that while they might be "hearing" what you're saying, they're just not ready to "listen." The good news is that even when someone isn't ready to listen, once they've heard your content it's in their brain where their subconscious will start considering it. So cut those distracted folks some slack and focus your attention on the participants who are engaged.

While you're at it, cut yourself some slack here too. No one is perfect in the beginning, and it's going to take a few experiences for you to figure out what feels good and works for you. You're stretching your comfort zone, so give yourself time to figure out what does and doesn't work. Give yourself permission to make mistakes along the way too. Trying to be perfect right out of the gate is a surefire way to stall your success! No one is perfect!

There are however, three easy ways to engage with your audiences that will hold their attention while also providing you with a chance to breathe. Obviously, using any or all of them depends on how long you're speaking for.

1. Ask questions and then give people the opportunity to contribute their answers.
2. Have people raise their hands to indicate yes or no, or to vote on something.
3. Give people reasons and opportunities to interact with each other.

The good thing about these strategies is that they all give you a bit of a break—even if it's just to take a sip of water.

The Big Advantages of Small Steps

With all the small steps you've been taking it won't be long before you start enjoying your time on stage. How do I know this? It's been one of the results I've experienced personally. But if you think about it, it makes perfect sense. If it didn't start feeling good to be on stage at some point, our world wouldn't have any actors, musicians, athletes, or teachers. And, if they can stand in front of others to share what they care about, so can we!

Another reason I know it's going to get easier is because the more you talk about your topic, the deeper your own understanding of it will become. You'll get better at sharing it each time you speak, which means you're confidence will grow each time you speak. Knowing more about your specific subject than your audience is a confidence boost too. Even when there are people in your attendance who are knowledgeable on your topic, you'll be sharing your content from your book's perspective, which means you're extremely likely to talk in ways that provides new insights and information.

Here's another small but nifty trick you can use that pays huge dividends. Did you know your brain can only think one thought at a time? Go ahead . . . try to think a positive and a negative thought at the same time. It can't be done. This is very cool because it means that if you're on stage and you realize you're about to get sidetracked by a fearful or negative thought—like the thoughts that might pop into your mind when you see someone in your audience laughing at something on their cell phone—all you have to do is to give your brain something else to think about. Shift your attention and focus to your outline to remind you of what's next, or find the friendly face of a person who has been paying attention and enjoy the feeling of the balance shifting back in your favor.

You can do other things too like sticking a couple of inspirational post-it notes where you can see them. If nothing seems to be working, I'm a fan of the "pause." Again, your audience won't know you're having a "moment" unless you tell them. So, if you suddenly realize there's "empty air," just turn it into a meaningful pause as if you are deliberately pausing to invite your audience to think about the value of what you just said. It will give you the time you need to take a steadying breath, remind yourself of why you're here, and reconnect with what's next on your outline. Pausing is a powerful technique that reminds us that we are in charge.

*****

Now it's time to think about how cool it is that you've reached this point! You might still feel a bit jittery just before you speak your first words, but even the most famous people on the planet admit to feeling nervous before they take the stage. So don't expect to stop feeling nervous altogether because you don't have to! Instead, know that what you feel about public speaking will evolve. It will stop being F.E.A.R. and turn into the feeling of excitement that comes with knowing you're about to help someone . . . probably a bunch of someones just by sharing information from your book with them.

So congratulate yourself! Take a moment to bask in the fact that you have something brilliant and meaningful to share, and that you have a stage to share it from. Look around the room and take a moment or two to breathe and feel gratitude for the opportunity to speak. Own the fact that you're going to rock the stage—in a positive and good way!

10

Post Speech Fear

I love the way Arnold Schwarzenegger delivered his signature tag line in the movie *Terminator II*: "Come with me if you want to live!" Translation: *You might have survived so far, but if you don't want to die, it's time to beat feet.*

What the heck does this have to do with speaking? Well, the first few times you speak you'll notice that as soon as you share your final words you're going to be in a bit of a daze. On one hand you're thrilled and excited to be finished. You're feeling good and thinking you might have done a good job— maybe even a great job. Congratulations are definitely in order. On the other hand you're probably feeling like you want to get off the stage and beat feet towards the nearest exit too. After all, why push it?

What happens after you're done speaking is going to be different depending on the group you're speaking to. If you're part of a meeting, then you might be leaving the stage as soon as you're done and that will be that. But most of the time when you're done speaking, there's a moment ready to unfold. Most often, this moment will unfold on its own... unless you cut it short by getting off the stage as quickly as you can. Don't do it.

Instead, get that moment rolling by taking a few seconds to look into your audience. Take a breath and smile while being grateful for the time you've had with them. Say "thank you" to them for giving you the opportunity to share your topic and your book with them. Do you have to say thank you out loud? Not necessarily. And now that you know this moment is going to take place every time you speak, you'll have plenty of time to think about what's going to feel right and natural for you. Will you mouth the words? Say them out loud? What about doing a modified bow? Will blowing them a kiss work? Hey ... a kiss wouldn't work for me, but there are plenty of speakers who it would work for! Are you one of them?

Would it surprise you to learn that they want to say thank you to you too? It shouldn't because of course they're grateful to you for taking the time to share information about you, your topic, and your book with them. And it's only polite for you to provide them with your time and attention while they do it. If it feels uncomfortable basking in the sound of their applause, at the very least, remember that the more grateful they are for what you've shared with them, the more likely they are to buy your book. So don't cut them off in mid-clap just because you're ready to stop being the center of attention!

On a technical note, if you're speaking at a formal event with a podium and there's an emcee running the show, proper speaking etiquette is to never leave the podium/microphone unattended. Instead, wait for the emcee to come back on stage and replace you at the podium. It might lead to another moment of attention and applause for you, but there are worse things in life to have to get used to!

The first few times you finally get off the stage, you might be looking for your next chance to escape. Once again, let me start by offering my heartfelt congratulations on your success! Remember way back in the day when you were convinced it was never going to happen? Seems like years ago now.

Anyway, no escaping here either because this is one of the easiest and most enjoyable parts of speaking—the one-to-one conversations you get to have with people after you've left the stage. This is when you get to meet and mingle with the people in your audience. It's when you can start building real relationships with people that will lead to book sales, networking, and more opportunities to speak too.

If you really, really, really, need to escape, take a quick but short trip to the rest room. Look at yourself square in the eye when you look into that mirror and congratulate yourself. Take some steady calming breaths, wash your hands, and get back out there and mingle! Trust me; there will be people who want to talk to you. It's normal. After all, they came to the event to see and hear you speak. So talk to them. This is your chance to give them your attention, which they will totally appreciate.

One of the beautiful benefits of exchanging pleasantries with your audience is that you're going to see, hear, and learn pretty quickly that you did just fine on stage. You did not stink, and from what people are saying, they enjoyed listening to you. How great will it be to hear that? Trust me when I say it definitely feels great.

There's an opportunity for another one of those "moments" to unfold here too. Knowing that people are waiting for an opportunity to speak with you directly is going to have you feeling a little bit like the rock star everyone wants to hang out with after the show. Make sure to appreciate and be grateful to and for each person. And remember, this is your chance to give them your attention in appreciation for the attention they gave you while you were on stage.

Now there's one must-do thing left to do. You need to find the person who booked you, or the person in charge of the event. The timing here is dependent on how the event has been set up. If you don't have a book sales table, you'll probably want to find this person when you're done mingling. If you do have a book sales table, you could talk to them before you go to your table, or after. The person in charge is usually the last one to leave the event, so there's room to get the lay of the land and then make your decision.

There are many reasons for seeking this person out, and plenty to cover during your conversation with them. With one exception, all of those reasons will be covered in the advanced book. But I'm betting you already know what the exception is without me saying it. And yup, I'm going to say it anyway. When you find that person, shake their hand, look them in the eye, and thank them for giving you the opportunity to speak to their audience.

That's it! You're done! Well, except for making sure that you sign every book that's been purchased. Actually, this is something you can think about beforehand too. How do you want to sign your books? Signing your name isn't all that exciting, so come up with a short message. It can be inspirational, personable without being personal, or whatever. Shorter is better so you can remember it rather than having to copy it—which won't give anyone the warm fuzzies. Try out different possibilities until you come with a signature phrase you like. Physically practice writing it beforehand too so you'll be used to working in the amount of space available in your book.

That's it!

Congratulations! You've made it all the way through your first public speaking gig! Okay, so maybe you've only done it in your mind, but that's where everything we do begins—between our ears.

Together, we've tackled and dissected the biggest public speaking fears people have. We've renamed them for what they really are—false evidence appearing real—and we've gone over simple and easy steps for pushing them out of the way.

We've journeyed all the way from you thinking about trying public speaking to the moment when you're done speaking, selling and signing your books, and it's time to pack up. It's been a good journey and I'm proud of you for sticking it out. It's proof that your book means something to you, which means it's likely to mean something to other people too. And now you know you can do this.

That's the whole reason you read this book—because you believe in your book enough to want to sell more copies so you can help more people. Well, that's the reason I wrote this book. I believe in your book too, and now that we've reached the shared conclusion that public speaking is going to help you accomplish this goal, it's time to move on to finding public speaking opportunities.

Part 4

11

Where to Find Speaking Opportunities

I wish I could tell you that finding speaking gigs when you're just getting started is easy, but there's no denying that securing your first few might be a challenge. Persistence is the key that will start opening doors for you, which means you're going to have to be willing to ask. In fact, in the beginning, you have to be willing to <u>persistently</u> ASK! ASK! ASK!

The good news is that there are literally thousands of meetings taking place every day that need speakers. So . . . if they need speakers . . . and you're willing to speak . . . I'm just saying. Granted, it's unlikely that small local organizations will pay you to speak. There are going to be organizations that won't let you actively promote your book from the stage either. But don't let those situations put you off because practice is practice. This is also how and where most speakers get their start—speaking to small local groups, clubs, and organizations.

There are also definite advantages to starting out this way:

- Most of the time you'll be speaking for 20 minutes or

less—which is a lot less stressful than speaking for an hour when you're just starting out.
- These gigs are usually easier to find.
- People don't expect you to be perfect.
- You will meet people who might know other groups you could speak to.
- Speaking to these groups is going to help you figure out your speaker comfort zone.

Most importantly, each time you speak you're speaker-skill level is going to rise, your confidence is going to grow, and your reputation as a good author-speaker will get around.

What kinds of groups, clubs, and organizations am I talking about? Civic organizations and churches for a start. There are plenty of local Chamber of Commerce, Rotary clubs, and local networking groups too. Think about the places where you've heard people speak. Would any of them be a good fit for you? One thing I know for sure is that they can't say yes if you don't ask—so ask!

How about local garden clubs, senior communities, and charitable organizations? Are there associations who might be interested in your topic?

Another thing I know is that when most authors start speaking they think that "everyone" could benefit from reading their book. So start thinking about where all your "everyones" are getting together. Once you start thinking outside the box, you'll be surprised what you'll find. I know this is true because I've spoken at a bunch of American Federation of Teachers (AFT) and American Federation of Labor and Congress of Industrial Organization (AFL-CIO) events.

Speakers are needed for lunch hour meetings. There are

businesses that bring in speakers to speak to their customers too. Hardware stores need speakers. Lumber yards do too. If you're a self-improvement expert you could speak at a tea shop or a boutique grocer. Non-traditional markets need speakers. Specialty stores need speakers. A speaker could speak at a car wash event, in a doctor's office, or at the bank. There are restaurant, ski lodge, movie theater, appliance store, and even coffee shop opportunities. This is just a small sampling of all the opportunities there are to speak.

Now, consider all the virtual opportunities there are to share your book and message with people around the globe! The point is that with just a little bit of effort and imagination, you'll never run out of people to call and ask about speaking opportunities. And then, while other authors are complaining about not being able to find anywhere to speak, your first speaking gigs will already be behind you.

Evidence

I understand you might think I'm just trying to make it sound better than it really is, so I did a quick internet search for associations because I know that associations host events that need and use speakers. I picked and clicked on Wikipedia's **List of Industry Trade Groups in the United States** and was rewarded with a list of close to 300 associations. Check it out and scroll through the list. I'm pretty sure you're going to see your niche or even micro-niche represented in a bunch of different places.

Don't let this list overwhelm you though. Like I said, I've just added it here as actual evidence of the fact that there are speaking opportunities everywhere. Also, there are strategies for mining lists like these, which is something I write about in the advanced book too.

Remember that this book is all about helping you prepare, secure, and get through your first speaking gigs. From there, you get to decide how much speaking you want to do. There's no rule that says you have to want to speak at national association meetings if you don't want to. Whether your goal is to speak on national or international stages, or stages within an hour's drive of your home, like every single other speaker, you have to start somewhere.

12

Conclusion

You know what? I've really enjoyed our time together in this book. I wrote it because I know how important it is for us to speak to share our books and message with other people. I get to experience how good it feels every time I take the stage and I want the same for you. I want you to know what it feels like when you get past the fear and start sharing your book and your message. There really is nothing like it.

So let's do a quick recap. Why should we, as authors, speak? Because we have a contribution to make. We have something important to say—something that's going to add to life's conversations. All we have to do is get past that first big hurdle, our fear of public speaking. Once we overcome that our reputation as an author-speaker will grow and people will start asking us to speak before we ask them. The result is more opportunities to fearlessly sell more books!

Getting started as a speaker might not be easy, but starting anything isn't easy in the beginning. If it were, anyone and everyone would do it. As an author, you already know what you're going to talk about and that puts you way ahead of people who don't have a good reason to do the work of getting past their fears. Still, remember that the decision to begin is yours to make.

Once you've made the decision to start, and then followed up that decision by coming up with a talk based on your book and expertise, it's time to let people know you're available to speak. Keep brainstorming for opportunities, and start working on your "ask" muscle by asking people if they know of anybody looking for speakers, or if they have any ideas for you.

If the idea of asking makes you feel uncomfortable, remind yourself of the people who are going to benefit from your book. They need your assistance. If they didn't, you wouldn't have had a reason to write your book in the first place! So while it can be uncomfortable to ask for a speaking opportunity when you're getting started, the temporary discomfort of asking is nothing compared to the feeling and experience of actually helping someone improve some aspect of their life. It is truly one of the most rewarding experiences a human being can have—not to mention something to be proud of.

Not in a gloating or boasting way though. It doesn't feel like that . . . well . . . not exactly like that. I'm not going to lie; when no one else is watching it feels like a victory that might be worthy of a little victory dance. But not like a competitive victory. It's more like a *"Yes! I did something good! I made a contribution! I contributed something meaningful that was all mine to contribute and someone's world is better for it!"*

Be proud of your contribution. And be proud of doing something most people can only dream of doing. Be proud of the work you've done to become a published author. Once you start speaking you'll have one more thing to be proud of too. Then focus your attention on gratitude for each and every speaking opportunity that comes your way, and of course, for all the books you're now selling!

Conclusion

You can become an author-speaker. It's not really any different than the decision you made to write your book and become an official author as a result. That was probably scary in the beginning too because you weren't sure if you could do it. But now you know you can write a book. And now that you've read this book and are better prepared to tackle the hurdles most speakers face, all you really need to do is get started.

I know you've got this and I sincerely hope you'll reach out to me and brag about how well your first speaking gigs went! And yes, I said "brag" because every new speaker should be able to brag about defeating all that **F**alse **E**vidence **A**ppearing **R**eal. I understand how good that feels and am here so you have someone to celebrate your "victory" with.

Authors Should Speak

Speaker Tips from Authors Who Speak

Author Speaker Tips

Julia Tannenbaum

As someone who struggles with an anxiety disorder, public speaking has always been a huge fear of mine. Just a few years ago, I was too scared to raise my hand in class, and whenever someone talked to me, I wouldn't look them in the eyes. In fact, until I published *Changing Ways*, even the idea of being able to confidently and comfortably speak in front of an audience was unimaginable.

But I had a story to tell, and I knew that in order to tell that story, I had to overcome my fear. I started small with book groups and close family members. I embraced my awkward personality and joked about my anxiety instead of trying to mask it. I reminded myself that people weren't innately evil, and therefore wouldn't judge me if I stumbled over a word or forgot a thought. Most importantly, I accepted that I wasn't, nor would ever be, perfect.

Today, I'm much more confident in my speaking ability. I've spoken to audiences of all different sizes and demographics, and although my anxiety persists, I know that as long as I apply my skills and keep a positive mental attitude, I'll be okay.

Julia Tannenbaum
www.wackywriter.com

Author of

Changing Ways

Brian Jud

Soon after publishing my first book I realized that I was not utilizing an important promotional tool, and that was to speak on my book's topic: How to get a job. Unfortunately, I had no experience speaking before groups and the thought of doing so was unsettling. Soon, the need to sell books overcame my reluctance.

My first task was to learn how to speak professionally, so I joined the New England chapter of the National Speakers Association. I attended meetings regularly and quickly learned the fundamentals. While applying my knowledge, I learned two things quickly. The first was to begin with small groups, and the second was to find ways to force myself to do it.

I began by speaking to groups of three or four people at various re-employment meetings. My audience sizes progressed to the point where I was regularly speaking to ten, then twenty or more people. In order to force myself to do this, I started a re-employment group at my church. We met weekly, and I had to speak before groups of 50 or more at times. This experience led to my speaking at state-run assemblies of 200 – 300 unemployed people. It also gave me the confidence to speak to audiences in the millions on national TV and radio shows.

I also recognized the need to speak before college students, a potentially lucrative segment for book sales. In order to force myself to do so, I became an instructor at a local university. This gave me practice as well as credibility when pursuing speaking events at other universities. I soon became comfortable speaking before hundreds of students at a time.

My recommendation? Study the craft of speaking and practice regularly. Build your self-confidence by speaking before small, then progressively larger groups. Most likely you will make some blunders but consider them learning experiences. After each presentation, evaluate your performance to see how you might improve. Your confidence will grow with each event and soon you will be looking forward to the opportunity to speak more often.

Brian Jud
brianjud@bookmarketing.com

Author of

How to Make Real Money Selling Books: A Complete Guide to the Book Publishers' World of Special Sales

Beyond the Bookstore: How to Sell More Books Profitably to Non-Bookstore Markets

Jane Herr Desrosiers

Top tip is to be prepared with how you will approach your topic. If you are speaking about your book, outline what got you to this very moment. From inspiration to publishing, people like to know the journey that you have been on. Your experience adds more depth to your conversation with your audience. And treat your presentation like a conversation. If there is a podium, step to the side and come closer to your audience. Try to become more at ease with them by asking them questions. Your ease will make the experience better for you and them.

Practice, record, or use whatever device to listen to yourself. Too many umms and your audience will take notice. Do you make a funny face when you're searching for the word? Have someone watch you.

Wear comfortable clothes. If you're tugging at your outfit or your shoes are tight, you'll subconsciously be thinking about that and not about your audience. They will also become acutely aware that something is bothering you.

If you wear glasses, wear the damn glasses. Vanity is for movie stars, glasses make you human.

And last, smile and say thank you. Without your audience, your opportunity for greatness never happens.

Jane Herr Desrosiers
www.janeherrdesrosiers.com

Author of

Gone Fishing The Hook
Gone Fishing The Line
Gone Fishing The Sinker

Chuck Miceli

Search the internet for people's top fears and you will consistently find that public speaking ranks right up there as number one or two. Add to that fact that many writers are introverts by nature and it is readily apparent why so many of us would rather be in the audience than in front of it.

I consider myself fortunate that my path to writing came out of my love for public speaking rather than the other way around. It was because of my frequent criminal-justice speaking engagements that I received a paid offer to research and write about deadly fires in prisons and jails. What was supposed to be a brief pamphlet for administrators became a 130 page manuscript. That manuscript was published as my first co-authored book, Fire Behind Bars, which led to many more public speaking events.

I have done hundreds of speaking engagements throughout the United States for groups from 4 to 400. Working on my fourth book, I still find writing more challenging than speaking. Several key factors have contributed to my public speaking comfort. I hope these suggestions will help you in your own efforts to promote what you publish.

Love Your Audience: This may seem a strange place to start, but for me, it is essential. Many public speaking phobias come from fear of rejection, ridicule or humiliation. The reality is that most people who come to hear you speak are there because they are genuinely interested in hearing what you have to say. If you've done your work in preparing for the presentation, then you have a gift for your audience and your speaking engagement is the opportunity to give it to them. Likewise, their attention is their gift to you. It's always a good idea to thank them for attending. Each time I speak, I remind myself of this and I suggest that you do the same.

Accept That You Will Not Please Everyone*:* Some people will not read fiction no matter how well written. Others love science fiction and have no use for romance. No book ever written has universal appeal to everyone.

The same is true for public speaking. No matter how gifted you are as a speaker, there will be people in the audience that will not resonate with you or your message and that is perfectly fine. Once you believe that, you are free to deliver your message to the best of your ability and accept everyone who attends, including those it does not reach.

If someone does challenge you, don't try to defend your position. Simply acknowledge their right to their own viewpoint. After doing so, I usually point out something I truly believe: "Not all of the knowledge rests with the person at the front of the room."

Consider Your Subject Matter*:* I believe that a great deal of public speaking anxiety comes from being uncertain about how our subject matter will be received. I also believe that a primary source of that anxiety stems from the approach of trying to decide what to tell the audience, rather than considering what they want to hear. Put yourself in an audience member's seat and ask yourself what you would want to hear. Then, build your presentation around meeting those expectations.

Prepare*:* You've probably heard the joke about the tourist who asked a stranger how to get to Carnegie Hall and the stranger replied, "Practice, practice, practice." The same is true for public speaking. I always outline my talking points; not every word, but each major point I will be stressing.

The problem with adding too much detail is that you wind up reading from your notes rather than talking to your audience. Jot down the major points and then, in your head, consider the details you will stress in your talk. Then, just as you do with your writing, go over your plan and refine it until you're satisfied. You can even practice by speaking it aloud and timing the presentation.

Use Slides Wisely: I frequently use PowerPoint slides with my presentations. Done properly, they can greatly enhance a presentation. Done poorly, they can be detrimental. Some points to consider include the following:

- The fewer words the better. The more words, the smaller the font and the harder it will be for your audience to read them, especially in larger rooms.
- Consider pictures instead of words. That will prompt you on what to say and not have your audience distracted by reading while you are talking.
- Don't use too many slides. If you have a thirty-minute talk, fifteen slides should be plenty. Too many slides and audience members get antsy wondering how many more before you finish. I sometimes number the slides starting with the highest number first and counting down to zero. That way, the audience knows exactly when we will be finished.
- Don't talk to the slides. If you have too much information on the slides, you might end up reading them instead of talking to the audience. Remember, they came to hear you.

Start on Time, End on Time: Remember that audience members have no control over the timing of your presentation; you do. They will very much appreciate the speaker who values their time by adhering to the posted schedule. If your presentation is supposed to start at 6:30, either begin promptly at that time, or explain to the audience why there will be a delay. Tell them when you will begin and then begin promptly at that time.

Likewise, if your presentation is scheduled to end at 7:30, end promptly at that time. For many people, questions are the most valuable part of the presentation. If you're going to invite questions, end a few minutes early and include them in the overall schedule. I will often announce that we have reached the ending time but for those who still have questions I will be happy to talk to them individually after we dismiss and I've finished signing books.

Constantly Improve: Understand and accept that, just like developing your writing or any other skill, you will not be an instant expert. As a wise friend of mine use to teach: *To master any new skill, you must "lean into your discomfort."* Accept your shortcomings and celebrate your growth. Ask yourself what and how you could improve the next time and incorporate that learning into your future presentations. When your presentation goes well, bask in the moment and congratulate yourself on your new growth and development.

That does it for me. Thank you for allowing me to share these ideas with you. I hope I have provided information that might help ease some of your own public speaking concerns. From my own experience, it remains one of my favorite parts of being an author. In time, I hope it will do the same for you.

Chuck Miceli
www.authorchuckmiceli.com

Author of

Amanda's Room

Elsa Kurt

When I began writing with intent to publish, I envisioned glorious days and nights hovering over a computer screen, typing with mad glee until the words "The End" magically appeared. Then, I foresaw book launches, events and signings, accolades and admirers, and lines of people waiting to meet the author. I'm happy to say much of that came true. I did the things, I became The Author.

The admirers and lines of people? Eh, not so much. Turns out, there are a lot of us wearing the "The Author" crown. I mean a lot. Those book signings and events are sometimes great... and sometimes a bust.

There was however, one consistent occurrence. At every event, at least one person approached me with a hesitant gleam in their eye. At first, I thought it was excitement at meeting me, The Author. It wasn't. It was because they wanted to share that they, too, have written a book (or always wanted to) but didn't know what to do next, or how.

Well, I thought, *I can help you!* I gave them all the info I could, answered their questions and cheered them on. Their excitement and gratitude intoxicated me. I didn't think, *Oh, my God, I can make money at this.* I thought, *I can help people pursue their goals.* But how does an introvert do something so extroverted?

I watched every motivational speaker I could find. I read books and took a course in public speaking. I had to figure out how this non-public speaking introvert could become a confident speaker. It was my husband who gave me the answer, and now the advice I give you.

***Talk about what you know,
your experiences, your passion.***

It was a light bulb moment. The fear abated (it never vanishes completely) and I sought opportunities to share my hard-gained knowledge, my mistakes and missteps, accomplishments, and my personal truths on the writing, publishing, and promoting journey. Because of this, I've launched several budding authors on their journeys (two of which honored me with book cover mentions). I still love writing most of all, but speaking is now a very close second.

Elsa Kurt
www.elsakurt.com

Author of

Mae's Cafe

Judith Dryer

I have to be honest. For me, getting the book written, edited and published was the hard part. The easier part (all relative here) was and is capturing nuggets from the book and creating presentations.

In the beginning of this process, my first rule of thumb for developing any presentation is to prepare and practice. I usually add a bit more content than I may need as a backup. Why? Some audiences will participate more, or an interview host will talk more than others. Those who are quieter may need a little bit of prodding or more examples. Either way, preparation reduces some of the stress of speaking.

Next, for some of my talks I use a PowerPoint slide presentation. Since I speak a lot in the Gardening, Sustainable Landscaping field, PowerPoint slides give a great visual. For example, a sterile landscape picture is so different from one filled with plant diversity. If a picture is worth a thousand words, I find PowerPoint to be a great aid. It also keeps me on track. I can highlight key points, understanding that about 60 slides gets me between an hour and an hour and fifteen minutes of presentation. It's also easy to tack on a few extra slides just in case.

I have participated in many book signing events at local libraries, book stores, craft fairs, farmers markets, etc. They are a great resource for connecting with folks who happen to be, or know, the person you can speak with to set up a talk. Many events have yielded several speaking engagements. Some when you least expect.

I am a Master Gardener, so I looked for organizations in my field and contacted them. Since I started doing this, I have been a keynote speaker at annual statewide meetings spoken at various organizations throughout New England and Virginia, and have been interviewed on radio and cable shows.

From this outreach, and using the content from my book, I have created four solid presentations, each with a different focus. Also, since I have taught holistic studies, I have developed three holistic-based presentations too.

I have also done talks without PowerPoint. I create an outline highlighting bullet points, try to engage the audience so they'll participate, and go from there. Knowing your material creates confidence too.

Lastly, practice reduces anxiety about public speaking. If you wrote a book, you know your material. I rarely receive a "no" when I contact a library or organization. They may be booked-out in advance, so you have to be proactive. Try Toastmasters if you want to polish your speaking skills.

There is no mystery here. Create a to-do list. Take daily action steps and before long you too will be a pro. To see all my class descriptions go to my website for more information.

Judith Dreyer
www.judithdreyer.com

Author of

At the Garden's Gate

ABOUT THE AUTHOR

Dan Blanchard is a best-selling author, an award-winning speaker, and an award-winning educator. Dan grew up as a student-athlete, and is a two-time junior Olympian wrestler who admits to being more of an athlete than a student. He is a double veteran who served in both the Army and Air Force, and has completed fourteen years of college, earning five masters degrees in the process. He is a two-time junior Olympian wrestling coach and currently teaches special education and social studies in Connecticut's largest inner-city high school.

Dan has given over 100 Toastmasters International speeches, over 100 public and professional speeches, and has been a guest on more than 100 radio, television, and podcast programs. In addition to the six books he's authored, he is featured in January Jones' book, *Priceless Personalities,* and Bill Corbett's book, *The Expert's Guide to Teenagers.*

In 2014, Dan was chosen by the American Federation of Teachers (AFT-CT) to be the face and voice of educational reform, and now represents the AFT-CT on the speaking circuit.

From the stage, Dan shares real-life lessons and inspiring stories with audiences of teens, adults, educators, and sometimes a mixture of all three. His goal is to positively influence the way we think about what is possible, regardless of how old we are or where we come from.

When Dan isn't in the thick of his professional pursuits, his time is devoted to his wife, their five children, and their home in Mansfield, CT.

Other Books by Dan Blanchard

The Storm: How Young Men Become Good Men

A Sprint to the Top: How to Win the Game of Life

The Evaluation of Professional Development in An Urban High School

Dan's Success Book for Kids!

A Teachers Guide to the Common Core

You can contact, connect, and follow Dan too:

www.DanBlanchard.net

Facebook:
www.facebook.com/daniel.blanchard.186

LinkedIn:
www.linkedin.com/in/daniel-blanchard-author-speaker-educator-and-tv-host-82a69723/

Twitter:
twitter.com/dan007blanchard   @dan007blanchard

Pinterest:
www.pinterest.com/dan007blanchard/

Instagram:
blanchard_dan

YouTube:
Dan Blanchard

Online On-demand Courses:
www.booksellinguniversity.com/courses/

Speaking for Authors, Beginner:

BSU – 103: Writers Should Speak: How Authors Can Share Their Message and Push Book Sales to the Next Level Through Speaking

Speaking for Authors, Advanced:
BSU – 103A: Writers Should Speak (Advanced Course)

What's Next?

If you liked this book and are ready to learn even more about being an author who speaks, be sure to check out Dan Blanchard's next book in this series:

Authors Should Speak: *How Authors Can Share Their Message and Push Book Sales to the Next Level through Speaking*

www.ingramcontent.com/pod-product-compliance
Lightning Source LLC
LaVergne TN
LVHW051841080426
835512LV00018B/3004